Mommy

The Hardest Job on Earth

Becki Pickett, M.C.P.

Copyright © 2021 Becki Pickett, M.C.P.

Cover design by Jeremy Glisson

Author photo by Judith Hill Photography

All rights reserved. No part of this book may be reproduced, distributed, stored in a retrieval system or transmitted in any form or by any means, without prior consent of the publisher. Client stories are compilations and aspects are not attributable to any identifiable person. The information in this book is not intended as a consultation and is not a substitute for evaluation by a health care professional.

ISBN: 978-1-7367542-5-2
Library of Congress Control Number: 2021909165

Capstar Publishing Dallas, TX

Dedication

This book is dedicated to all who accept this job however you decided to be a mom and however your child came to you.

There is no finer purpose.

Table of Contents

Introduction — vii

Part One: You — 1

1. Here you Are — 3
2. What Do YOU Want? — 21
3. Legacy & How to Build One — 41
4. Wiring & Why It Matters — 53
5. Location & What it Means — 61
6. Relationships & How They Work — 69
7. Who ARE You? — 85
8. Mommy Missions, Mantras, & Mandates — 101
9. Call in the Reinforcements — 113

Part Two: Babies, Toddlers, & Preschoolers, Oh My! — 123

10. Little Ones — 125
11. Sleeping — 139
12. Feeding — 145
13. Developmental Skills — 149
14. Fun & Games — 153
15. Temper Tantrums & Melt Downs — 161
16. Acting Out — 167
17. Relationships — 173
18. Fighting — 179

Part Three: Fly, Baby Fly 193

19. Leaving The Bubble — 195
20. Feels Like You've Got This! — 207
21. Sibling Rivalry — 211
22. Tweener Limbo — 221

Part Four: Teenagers 231

23. Invasion of the Body Snatchers! — 233
24. Same Partner, Different Dance — 245
25. It's Not Their Fault — 273

Part Five: Grown Up to Grown Up 283

26. Leaving the Nest — 285
27. Love the One They're With — 295
28. When Your Child Has a Child — 311

Part Six: When You've Got A Problem 321

29. How We Got Here Together — 323
30. Start Here — 333
31. Your Words Matter — 339
32. Coping Smart. — 345
33. Get Out from Under the Stress — 373
34. Hallelujah! — 383

Acknowledgements — 387
About the Author — 389
Contact — 391

Introduction

I was sure this title would grab your attention.

Every human being can relate. Instantly it brings emotion.

Think about it. In music there are only twelve notes and they account for every song ever created from classical to jazz to rock to rap. The entirety of the power of music from the beginning of time is expressed in those few notes.

Mommy says it all in five letters.

The Hardest Job on Earth sums up the impact of all the emotion you feel when you hear it. This is heart and soul stuff. And sweat and tears.

How'd you get here in this land of Mommy? Like most of us, you probably looked at the plump, pink-cheeked, sweet face of someone else's baby and said, *I want one of those!*

Babies are adorable.

They're miraculous and awe-inspiring. Let's face it, one of the most fabulous things in the world is the sweet smell of a baby's head. And how about those tiny smiles that turn up that little bit on one side of their mouth for the first time? Is there anything more heavenly blissful than a sleeping infant?

But they're also intimidating, demanding, and down-right scary. And that's before they can talk!

They come into the world so new, and their story is untold. They're also completely helpless and dependent and needy. But before you know it your tiny creature begins to evolve and emerge into an individual with a personality and likes and dislikes and even an opinion.

There are some really great humorous books out there about the wacky world of mommyhood. Relatable moms right in the middle of this job now are blogging and podcasting and writing some really funny stuff. I love that. Let's face it you do a lot of ridiculous things in getting this job done. And you feel like you're losing your mind in the process.

Having your peers who are experiencing this life phase along with you validate your feelings is so reassuring. You're not alone. Somebody's feeling the same way and it's okay. But then there are times when you realize feeling better about yourself isn't the only thing you need. What are you going to do to get this job done?

Introduction

You need advice that makes a difference in your child's outcome. You're responsible for not just what happens now and getting through this phase or even today but how your child turns out. You're shaping someone's life.

So, when you look to the experts for the serious stuff, you find all sorts of clinical advice, empirical evidence, and antidotal opinion. Statistics can rattle you to your core. The news about childhood mental health especially since the pandemic is getting bleaker and scarier all the time. Suicide attempts in teenage girls was up over fifty percent in 2020.

I know. It's so scary.

Then there's the advice of your mom elders. The moms who have done this the generation or two before you want to help because they've been where you are. But I know it feels pointless to get that advice from someone and to say *yeah, but you don't know what it's like to be a mom* NOW.

Today's moms, modern moms, I say *now moms*.

I have been a now mom when there wasn't a global tribe to help, and I had to figure it out as I went. I've been counsel to lots of people helping them restore their emotional equilibrium while parenting. I'm a daytime caregiver grandmother assisting a now mom in the middle of three modern childhoods as you are reading this.

Mommy

That puts me smack in the middle of my mom job.

I've been where you are.

I'm where you're headed.

I'm paving the way.

Here's what I want you to know.

This is a job for life.

Once you become a mom you never stop. Your kids can be any age, but they are still your kids and you're their mother, and those dynamics are ever changing. The ground is ever shifting. You never stop learning.

So that makes us all now moms.

Because I know the territory and because I see you struggling to get your job done successfully, I decided to write this book.

I have a lot of information for you backed by knowledge and fortified with experience. It's the trifecta of wisdom. I'm about finding answers and about passing them on. I love educating and explaining. Over the years I have found that simplest is often

Introduction

the most effective. There is an elegance in the economy of words when well chosen.

I'm here to tell you the steps you need to do this job in three simple words.

Are you ready?

Wait for it.

Here it is.

Handle with care.

It really comes down to that. But it encompasses a lot of work on your part. And a lot of thought and intent.

You're going to have to figure out what kind of care your child requires. If you have multiples you know that means, you'll need more than one method.

You've probably heard some version of the following.

Kids come in two varieties, orchids and dandelions.

That simple statement really does sum up the grab bag of parenthood. You get what you get. Some kids are easier, and some

Mommy

are harder, and you learn as you go. More importantly, it's a call to action.

I know that God is smart enough to give you what you need.

I know you're smart enough to figure it out.

That's why you're reading this.

To witness your child become a fully formed functioning human being contributing to the world is a life-long roller coaster ride.

You'll feel your heart soar when the wind is blowing your hair and the sun is shining and you're coasting along.

The next minute you'll feel your stomach bottom out on a hairpin curve in a storm you didn't see coming.

You'll feel like throwing up.

It's okay. It will pass and you'll get your land-legs back.

It will thrill you again.

And again.

And again.

Introduction

There are academic books about the first years of life and the developmental milestones to use as markers. There are behavior specific advice books for every possible subject for the problems that arise. There's a lot of territory to cover. We're talking about the formation of a complete human. We're talking about somebody's future here.

We're also talking about your life and your future.

This book recognizes, validates, and honors both. I knew I had to write it because I see the struggle. I hear the noise of so much information buzzing and see that somehow, it's not always landing.

I've worked with people as they learn to problem-solve and manage the stress of any difficulty. In that pursuit, I have come to realize that our choices all circle back to childhood in some lasting way.

It hurts my heart to see children receive less than they are owed, and it pains me to see moms miss the experience they deserve.

So, I decided to write this book using my Master of Counseling Psychology and all the psychological based information about behavior and emotions and childhood development I've learned. As well as the deep understanding from listening to the stories of individuals struggling with these issues. That's my professional contribution.

Mommy

The best I have to offer is my rock-solid convictions from being a mom.

Let me say this right here right now.

I do not have perfect kids.

Like unicorns, perfect kids don't exist.

The belief that they do and that you can create them is also a myth.

So is the idea of a perfect mother.

How much you're willing to do to get the job done in a way that sets your child up for success and happiness is the only measurement that counts.

What you get in return is the joy of a confident well-balanced person surrounded by support and love who believes that they deserve it.

What better evidence could there be for a job well done?

What better gift can you give your child and yourself?

Mommy is a job. The hardest job on earth hands down. It is wide and deep, and the heights are formidable but dazzling.

Introduction

People are different in as many ways as there are raindrops. That's why there as many answers to the question of what's best for each child. Accepting that it is a kinetic ever-evolving process is your best place to start. I will give you some tried and true suggestions and help you gain the confidence that you are the one with your best answer.

Kids ARE like mythical unicorns in the ways they are magical and mystical and marvelous.

And they do spread glitter in your life.

You think of kids in terms of phases and stages and I'm going to cover all those. I want you to think of yourself being in the same phases and stages but from your perspective as an adult. Your child is growing and changing and so are you. Understanding that and expecting it are crucial for your enjoyment of this process so I'm going to help you gain some useful insight and give you specific steps and suggestions.

I also recognize that you may not be a biological mom. You may identify as mom to your child. You may be the only parent in your child's life and the role is yours to fill.

I honor your commitment whatever the circumstance.

This book is about loving a child and providing for their physical,

Mommy

mental and emotional needs and desires with every intention as a nurturer. You'll hear me say the phrase *soul stuff* often. You won't find that term in any academic book. It's my way of distinguishing the intangible and intrinsic aspects of humanity that give them value. These are the gifts that are yours to give.

Loving a child with maternal strength is a mighty force that requires a mighty fierceness.

Mom might.

It's a superpower for sure.

You already have the big answers inside you and the immeasurable ability to do this job fabulously. I'm going to keep reminding you of that. I'm also here to fill in the blanks when you aren't sure of the answers.

You need successful strategies.

I want you to know *what* and *why* whenever you can. And I want to help you be okay when why can't be answered. What's next is more important.

That goal is two-fold. I'm going to give you problem-solving strategies that will offer you direction and restore your emotional equilibrium when stress wears you down. The best part is you'll

Introduction

be equipped to pass these great coping skills to your child to help them face whatever life throws their way.

So here it is. Ta-da! *Mommy; The Hardest Job on Earth*. I call it a mom manual because we all need instructions and the best ones come complete with a trouble-shooting guide for possible solutions.

So, get ready. Take your seat and buckle up. I want you to be glad you've chosen to take this wild and wonderful roller coaster ride.

PART ONE:

YOU

CHAPTER 1

Here you Are

Through-out your life you have choices to make. You can change schools, friends, hairstyles, your weight, the shape of your nose, your hair color, lovers, spouses, houses, and bosses.

The decision to become a mom doesn't have an exit clause. No do-overs.

You've probably said *nobody told me it was going to be this hard.*

There are days you wish you could snap your fingers and your child is grown and all the worries and concerns are done.

But look what you'd miss.

You know in your heart that it's worth it.

Like in any relationship you give up things in return for having the other person in your life. You choose a partner with the idea that the fun part of the dating game is over. Choosing a career means

Mommy

deciding on a path that puts other worthy pursuits aside. In the case of kids, you give up personal priorities from the ability to go to the bathroom alone to uninterrupted sleep to the summer home in Tuscany you always dreamed of that is preempted by the financial demands of braces and college tuition.

But before you panic at the enormity of it all, remember that everything in life is an adventure and you can't comprehend it all or you'd be too overwhelmed to do it.

Growing up, leaving home, going to college and or getting a job, living on your own, finding a partner, and all the other things in between and beyond are wonderfully unknown at the beginning. And scary. But you do them because of the reward.

I bet when you read the cover of this book you had one of two reactions.

If you've been a mom for a while it was probably a mental high-five.

Amen, sister!

If you're a brand-new mom, it was understandably a wave of anxiety.

Oh, crap!

Here you Are

Wherever you are on your mom road you're trying to figure out what to do next the best way you can. There's so much you need to know about so many things.

You might be asking yourself why you don't know the answers. After all, you're a very smart person. You may have a degree or a couple of degrees. You probably have a career going, a relationship, a life. You pay bills and rent or a mortgage and manage your money and maybe even some investments.

You are able-bodied and capable.

Billions of people have been moms for millions of years. Why do you need advice when this is a natural part of life? Doesn't all of it just come to you once you have a child?

And what about all the advice that is already bombarding you from every direction? Your mother, mother-in-law, grandmother, sister, friends, co-workers, neighbors, grocery store clerks, and strangers in the mall all have thrown in their opinion.

Even celebrities are telling you how to do this.

Everyone is full of information and they have no problem giving it to you.

Unsolicited.

Mommy

Now you're confused which is good advice and what is useless and what is relevant and what is old-fashioned and outdated for your now mom sensibilities.

This subject is no different than anything else in life in the way it evolves over time to some degree or the other. Experts gather more research results. Medicine and education provide innovation and invention and knowledge. That means pediatricians are changing the "rules" all the time for what's best.

Always place infants on their back. My new mom days.

Always place infants on their stomach. My daughter's new mom days.

Place infants on their back. Today's moms. See how it goes round?

Introduce solids at six months. My new mom days.

No solids until a year. My daughter's new mom days.

Peanut butter and more peanut butter. Me as a new mom.

No peanut butter. They might develop an allergy. Advice to my daughter.

Here you Are

Introduce peanut butter early to avoid allergy. Today's prevailing advice.

Sometimes trends and practices change as quickly as the time between your own kids.

School is very different now than when you attended.

Being a kid has changed.

Issues have shifted.

The flow of information never stops.

You expect other things in the world to change and evolve so you need to expect the same for this job.

In my lifetime there have been helicopter moms, tiger moms, hands-on moms, stay-at-home moms, working moms, home-schooling moms. Now there are badass moms, mompreneurs, momagers, and boss moms.

That's all to say you've got to keep up. But how do you not get caught up in following trend? And what about intuition? Aren't there some things you just *know?*

When my oldest was a newborn I took her into the pediatrician for

Mommy

a regular check-up. He asked how things were going and I began my reply with words of doubt that what I was reporting was correct. He stopped me abruptly and assured me with words I will never forget and will always be grateful to him for giving.

> *"No one knows this baby like you do. You are her mom expert. Whatever you tell me, I will believe because you know her better than anyone."*
>
> *−Joe Donaldson, M.D. (world's greatest pediatrician)*

I can't adequately express the confidence he gave me that day and every day after. He steeled me with a resolve that *I did* know her better than anyone else on the planet and I could be trusted to know what was right for her. It would be the foundation of my ability to make tough decisions and to resist self-doubt in my parenting responsibilities for the years to come.

Let me give you that gift.

Trust yourself.

You will have days you don't feel like you know anything. You are lost or confused or too tired to muster that confidence. But

Here you Are

every expert knows that knowledge is an on-going process. To be excellent you must continue to ask questions and seek answers.

The landscape will change as your child grows up. Each child will bring different experiences. The phases of your life will bring different rewards and challenges. That's why you must remain curious and open. The variables will shift but the love remains.

Some aspects of parenting are universal. You want your child to live a good life and be happy. Every generation has wanted the same. It's their everyday methods that differ. That's where you gather information and make the decisions for yourself.

You've decided to bring another human into your world. One day they'll go out into the world. You're making decisions for them now as well as yourself that will be lasting.

You hear a lot about teachable moments.

Let me tell you now that *every* moment you spend with them, you're teaching your child something. They're always observing. The big issues and the nuances of everyday life.

Life skills.

It all starts with you.

Mommy

Now before that wave of anxiety comes on you again, I want you to do something I'll ask you to do often as we talk together.

When it all seems too big or too difficult to look at in the moment, change the view.

It's like taking a selfie on your phone camera. Choose a filter that gives you an enhanced and more desirable picture. That's not denying reality. That's discerning with perspective.

Give it some sparkles.

Think of this mom job another way. With the responsibility comes the freedom for you to choose what you want to do. You get to create the life you want and be the mom you want to be.

You're in charge.

I will say that to you over and over

The way you approach this job, the way you fulfill your commitment, the way you feel about yourself, and the way you project all of that to your child is crucial.

You are your child's first role model.

You're their influencer!

Here you Are

This is to say I believe you have good parenting instincts already in you. You simply need someone to help you tap into that innate knowledge.

No matter where you are on the Mommy road, I will help you pinpoint your location and give you age and stage appropriate guidance for both you and your child. You're both going to grow along the way so let's get you going and growing in the same direction.

This relationship you're in is symbiotic and inseparable.

You are your child's taproot.

That's why I started this book with *You*.

Meeting your needs supplies theirs. In turn your desire to do it well is satisfied.

I get it.

Let me tell you right here and now.

I love this job.

I became a mom in my early twenties. I adored that time in my life. It wasn't always a picnic. My husband traveled hundreds of days out of the year for their entire childhoods, so I did this job solo

Mommy

physically. I say I lived the life of a single parent, but I didn't get to date! So, I know how taxing this job is when you're alone. Blessedly I had his unwavering support for all the decisions I made. He was my emotional high-five.

I recommitted myself again years later and took the job of daytime caregiver for my three very small grandchildren. It was a choice.

My friends thought I had lost my mind. I however, felt alive and fulfilled. I personally never feel more in touch with my humanity than when I'm mentoring a small child.

I've done this job and I'm still doing it. I want you to know how fully I recognize how tough it is and the enormity of it all.

It's tedious and boring and exhausting.

Then there's the immeasurable soul-filling love.

Since we're getting to know each other, you're about to discover I'm a cheerleader at heart. The caveat is I have a thing about vague positivity that reads like greeting cards and generic journal affirmations. I'm about finding genuine, honest-to-God celebration anywhere and anytime you can and using it as fuel to keep you going.

We're going to do that a lot together. I encourage you to learn

Here you Are

the value of celebration and use it often long after you've read this book. A little applause can go a long way for your emotional well-being.

It's like a dopamine and serotonin cocktail.

It's the antidote to the part of reality that sucks.

More important in many ways is the fact that celebration is also a great practice to teach your child. When they hear you celebrate yourself, they will emulate that behavior and will do the same for themselves.

Wow. Think about that for a moment.

Every time you applaud yourself, you're giving your child the tools that they need for building their self-esteem.

You are teaching them to love and value themselves.

I hope you'll see throughout this book how what benefits your child benefits you in return.

If you're a mom-to be, let me first say this.

YAY! I'm SO excited for you!

Mommy

I know firsthand these feelings that keep rushing over you. You're so excited you can hardly stand the anticipation. You're so overwhelmed with anxiety about all the unknowns that you can't let your mind wander. You feel brave and powerful then in the next moment you're scared to death.

Here's the upside to that. You have the luxury of preparation time. Before your life becomes a blur of baby frenzy, you have time to think about these strategies I'm going to lay out for you. Taking time to think is another fabulous coping skill. Many missteps can be avoided, and your emotional energy can be conserved by taking a small amount of time to give some thought to what you're feeling and what your options are for any situation before you react.

If you're a newbie mom, your hormones and your emotions are fluctuating like crazy. You're overwhelmed in a fog of new-mommy brain and need some reassurance and more information.

That's what I'm here for.

If you've been on this job awhile and have a child or multiples, you have encountered some challenges and issues, tried some of the advice you've been given, and used a trial-and-error approach. It's never too late to begin to take a look at where you are in the process and make a plan for where you want to go, who you want your child to become, and who you are in the picture.

Here you Are

It is never too late to start.

I am a big believer in preparation as protection. Let me say that again.

Preparation is protection.

You can't prepare for everything that happens in life. That's why you must prepare whenever and wherever you can. You do this in your career. You study, you train, you anticipate you make preparations, and you continue your education when needed to grow in your knowledge base to stay relevant and viable in an ever-changing world.

The same is true with this job.

When children are small and needy there are days that seem so long that they feel like eternity. Know that this will pass into memory in a blink. You've heard that a hundred times before but believe it. Remember when you thought you'd never be old enough to drive, finish school, get that degree, get a foothold in your career, find the right partner?

My first child was born a few months before my twenty-first birthday. Two years later I was a young mother of two babies nineteen months apart. My husband was traveling for work. I remember sitting in a rocking chair at two o'clock in the morning with a cherubic

Mommy

sleeping toddler draped across my lap and a beanbag newborn nestled on my chest. We lived in a rural area twenty minutes from the nearest city. It was a newly developed street and there were no streetlights. I had no idea how dark night could really be or how alone I could feel until then.

It had been one of those days where the hours had crept, and my stamina waned. My toddler was back to waking up in the night and the newborn was doing that newborn every couple of hours thing. I had finally gotten both little ones to sleep at the same time only to realize I was physically unable to stand up to carry either to bed without waking one or both of them. There was no one in the house to help me. I was so tired I could hardly stay awake. I knew I couldn't let myself go to sleep or I would drop both of them. My only thought was that at only twenty-two my life as I had known it was never going to be the same.

I was right. It was forever altered. Some changes were as simple as sleepy nights, and some were more difficult matters of the heart. What also happened that night was I realized that moment was just that. It was only a moment.

As I kept rocking until the sun came up, I envisioned them dressing themselves, going to the refrigerator to get their own cup of juice, dropping them both off at preschool and waving good-bye as I drove away for an entire morning spent reading the stack of magazines I had been saving.

Here you Are

That wasn't a fantasy.

It was clarity.

The time when they were no longer totally dependent was in front of me and I was already moving toward it. The key was to know that not now didn't mean not ever.

I tell you this very ordinary story because it is just that. No trauma, no catastrophic event, simply a mom moment. In that moment it felt big to only me. I want you to remember that it isn't about comparing your situation to anyone else's. It's about feeling what you feel without piling guilt on top.

You will have these moments.

It's okay to have these moments.

These moments will be memories soon.

This is about you and your child and I want you to know just like any job this one has highlights and lows.

It brings rewards and recognition and yet many times your work is taken for granted and goes unnoticed. Sometimes you have to drag yourself out of bed and make yourself go to work. You live for a vacation. You know that's true for a paid job so accept it in

Mommy

this one as well. But just like any career, you're building on your experience and acquiring skills through practice. The more you do it the better at it you become.

The difference here is you live with this boss 24/7!

You are their first power source. Let's amp it up so you have plenty to give without depleting yourself in the process.

Of course, I encourage you to take moments for yourself when possible.

Let others help you.

Go to the spa when you have a chance, even if it's only your own bathtub!

Don't feel guilty when you do have an opportunity to do something for yourself but don't beat yourself up when you can't find a way.

There's a way to have what you do for your child actually recharge you.

Yep, you heard me right.

You may feel exhausted but your beautiful, amazing brain never

Here you Are

stops thinking even if it's thinking a thought that says it can't think at all.

As long as you're alive you'll have millions of thoughts.

Let's make them work for you.

By the time you finish this book, you'll be using that like a superpower.

I champion you!

Let's do this!

CHAPTER 2

What Do YOU Want?

In the beginning, it's all about asking what your child wants. They cry. Do they want their diaper changed? Do they want to eat? Do they need a blanket? Do they want to be held?

As a toddler or small child, do they want green beans or carrots? Do they want to wear the Batman shirt or the Spiderman?

As a big kid, do they want the video game more or the new basketball hoop? Do they want you to wave good-bye when they get out of the car at school or pretend like you don't know them?

As a young adult, do they want your advice about their girl/boyfriend choice? Do they want your help figuring out where they should live? Or which job they should take?

Is anybody asking what YOU want?

Mommy

Wherever you are in your life as a mom you're always waiting for and expecting something specific to happen. That's just a way of saying you have preconceived ideas about outcomes. They're based on what you *want* to happen. It's the picture in your mind of how it should go.

Those expectations influence everything you do and how you react in situations.

Let's get you some clarity about yours.

I'll suggest you write or talk about what you're thinking as we go. You decide. There's space to jot notes right here on the pages of this book, or use your own journal, or simply talk out loud as you think about your answers to the questions I'll ask.

I'm a writer so I adore metaphors and similes. There's nothing like a good analogy for clarity. It helps when you're lost and need to identify where you are in a situation and need direction to get to where you are going especially when you're stuck.

They're also invaluable at getting your point across to others.

Here's a great opportunity to use one now.

Ready?

What Do YOU Want?

*When you find yourself up the proverbial sh*t creek without a paddle, use a metaphor or a simile to tread that water and get moving forward!*

So, as we talk use some images to move your mind toward your goals.

Let's go deep right off the bat. Think about this.

What do you want to happen?

Okay, if you're pregnant, I know this is a cliché question. I mean after all they call it expecting a baby. That's more of a description of your physical state.

But what's your state of mind?

Big one, right? This is for all moms to consider whatever your child's age. As soon as you found out you were going to be a mom you probably thought about your own childhood, the good parts and the parts that might not have been so great. You probably thought about your own mom and the kind of relationship the two of you have.

When you are in the middle of raising a child, you'll often think

Mommy

of how your mother did her job. You'll think in terms of what she did you agreed with and what you wish she had done differently.

This isn't blame time, it's discovery time.

How do you see yourself being a mom? This is so important.

It is the beginning of your child's childhood.

It's their legacy you're starting. But it began long before this. Your vision of parenthood is based on your childhood experience. If you're fortunate enough to have had a great childhood, then this will be easy to think about. If not, it might be painful to relive but it's the first step in assuring your child has better.

Let's talk about expectations in general. You already know they can be goals, objectives, projections or worthy fantasies to strive to achieve in your life. Have you ever thought about the fact that they're defined by the emotions they bring? Those desired emotions are what motivate you and move you toward happiness. Everyone has their own idea of what they believe will make them happy. You've heard the phrase *different strokes for different folks*.

Nothing could be truer.

Happiness is a wide-open space. You have all sorts of choices for the direction you choose to move you toward it. Your comfort

What Do YOU Want?

zone may be vastly different than most people or it might be quite common. What you see for yourself is your perspective based on your beliefs.

You've heard the experts ask, *what makes you happy?* That's a very hard question to answer in concrete terms. It's easy to default to the cliché beauty pageant answers of world peace and love that are admirable but don't really target you and your everyday life. But your answer matters.

Often when asked what makes you happy, you shrug and struggle for a definitive definition. Take it further and consider that unease is caused by uncertainty. Uncertainty leads to confusion and discontentment that can then morph into a general dissatisfaction in life because you can't quite define it.

You've also heard the phrase *you've got to name it to claim it.*

Boom!

That's so true.

Where do you begin to figure it out? In deciding what will make you happy or how you will succeed at any task you start with questions. There are basics to cover with the why, what, when, and how questions. I believe another crucial component is once you consider

Mommy

those questions to ask yourself what you expect the outcome to be. That's the directional guide for you to execute your plan.

Now that you have a child in your equation, they become central in your formula for happiness. They are a constant variable that can alter everything and affect the outcome.

Whether you are expecting a baby, or your child is a newborn, or whether they're grade schoolers, teens, or young adults, let's talk about what your expectations are as of this moment in your life and theirs.

You probably had a picture in your mind of what your child would look like before they were born. Then they might have surprised you with their curly hair or green eyes when you were expecting to see your straight locks and their dad's brown eyes.

The same is true of temperaments and personalities. You might get a child who isn't anything like you expected. You thought they would be just like you and they had the nerve to be like someone else altogether!

Maybe when you get one child figured out and think you've got a handle on this parenting thing, another child comes into your life and throws all of that out the window.

About the time you think you're pretty good at it, you get hit with

What Do YOU Want?

a moment that convinces you that you have no idea what you're doing. How well you deal with those surprises is directly related to your expectations.

Your expectations are the blueprint of your parenting style. They will influence everything.

Where did you get your expectations? What exactly are yours?

No matter the age of your child, taking a look at you is a great start. Begin with what you already know. You can build from there. Think about what you loved about your childhood and what would you wish had been different. What you expect is a great baseline to begin mapping out your child's legacy.

- Do you expect to repeat or reset the environment of your childhood as a parent?

- Are you expecting to be like your mom or are you aiming to be a different kind of mother?

- Do you expect your child to bring the things you feel you may have missed into your life?

- Do you expect your child to bring their own agenda to your life or simply adapt to yours?

Mommy

- Are you expecting the relationship you have with your child to change with time?

- Are you expecting recognition and gratitude for the efforts and sacrifices you are making and will make?

- Do you expect your relationship with your spouse or partner to remain the same once you begin to parent together?

- Can you and your parenting partner agree on your expectations as parents of each other?

- Can you and your partner agree on your expectations of your child?

- Are you expecting to love your child unconditionally?

I have to take this moment to talk about the concept of unconditional love. That phrase is used so often, but I don't think the reality of the practice matches the concept where humans are concerned. Does that surprise you? You're saying, *Becki, of course I love my child unconditionally. There's no way I could love them more.*

Take a moment to consider another way to think about it.

The concept of unconditional love isn't about *quantity*.

What Do YOU Want?

It's about *value*.

Love is transactional.

You give with an expectation of reciprocity.

It is the currency of love. You love with the goal of receiving the same. You give to get. You may not believe the other person will love you back, but it is your hope, your intent to motivate them to do so. If they do, you expect them to return your love, to nurture it, and protect it in ways equal to what you give. They expect you to do the same. It's a love transaction.

Think about it, you ask your child to behave, to stay out of trouble, to be responsible and trustworthy, to make their grades, to be a good person. You still love them if they get off track but your affection toward them may be hard to maintain while they are not complying with your requests or expectations. When the conditions aren't met then difficulty and conflict set in.

That sounds like something that shouldn't be said out loud, but it's a truth you need to acknowledge. The guilt you feel when you are at odds with your child will fester and spread into all parts of your relationship. It will make you question your abilities.

There'll be times when you have to dig through the disappointment and go deep to tap into the foundational love. Isn't that true

Mommy

about your relationship with anyone else in your life? Your partner makes you angry or your friend fails to support you, or your parent remains hard to get along with and the resulting frustration colors your perception of the relationship. The love is still there but the compatibility wanes.

You'll feel this with your child at times.

I think rather than unconditional what you and all of us are really seeking to give and receive is *unlimited love*. The scope of love that has no bounds as far as amount. You want loyalty, got your back, steadfast and unshakeable love that remains *regardless* of circumstance, or time, or your performance. The kind that stands united against pain with courage and alongside suffering with deepest empathy.

Love should rejoice and replenish.

There is no greater feeling than to know that someone's heart soars with you in the moments of happiness and still loves you despite your shortcomings and deficits.

Whole-hearted love runs soul deep.

Every child deserves that kind of love.

YOU deserve that kind of love.

What Do YOU Want?

Being a mother is the perfect incubator for that love to grow.

It's the *safe* place for it to grow.

It can protect against the bumps and cushion the blows.

You lay the foundation.

You provide the shelter.

You set the ground-rules,

You make your deal-breakers clear.

You provide protection.

You're now in a parent-child relationship. You're the leader. You're setting the example for how it will grow and evolve and be passed on generationally.

I know you love your child. How do I know? Because you are making an effort to learn, to discover, and to nurture. That's the foundation of your relationship. Remember that love is the catalyst, the motivation, the cornerstone, the sustainer, the essential ingredient of this relationship.

Mommy is your opportunity to have and to give all of that.

Mommy

Preparedness is the first step to knowledge.

Knowledge leads to clarity.

Clarity leads to successful action.

You have expectations from the moment you know you're a mom. You have a picture in your mind of how this will go. If your child is already here, then the one thing you've found is often times all doesn't go according to plan.

Make a list of what you want to happen. This is where you give yourself a reality check. Think in terms of reasonable expectations. These are the basics that you can supply. Those must be in place first and are the things your child should count on from you. They are reasonable because they are easily obtained. They are logical by assumption. Your child should be able to assume you will provide them with what they need. They expect if of you. You expect to supply them as part of your commitment.

Then think of expectations as the prospects that can occur with certain probability through your actions. What does that mean? The things you can insure will happen. You set out to make them happen with your efforts.

Your reasonable expectations are the solid foundation for your

What Do YOU Want?

child's dreams. Certain things need to be in place. Think of them as the baseline.

I urge you to reevaluate your expectations from time to time. Jot your thoughts down as you ask yourself these questions for some clarity. Think about your earliest mom expectations then what you're expecting now.

The Expectation Evaluation.

- Was your original expectation workable?

- Was it reasonable?

- Is it still reasonable and workable?

- Is there something you can adjust to make it more likely?

- Is it still relevant?

- Does your expectation need a tweak?

- Has that expectation been replaced by another one?

- Can you think of another reasonable expectation to put in its place?

Mommy

- Was your expectation centered on your child?

- Is it still fulfilling that purpose?

- Can you be open to expecting some your expectations to change when needed?

- Are you willing to allow your child's desires to shape your expectations?

This doesn't mean you have to limit your dreams for your child, but it does mean you need realistic and obtainable intentions first. Then you can think of the vision board of your child's life. Now that you know more about who they are in terms of their personality and temperament you can see their interests and aptitudes beginning to take shape. What are your wildest dreams for them? What are their dreams? The beauty of dreams is that they don't have to be reasonable or rational. Once you have the basics in place then the foundation is strong enough to support anything. You can help build toward those with that same intention.

That is the real reward that awaits you. Your happiness will follow your child's. Don't let anyone tell your differently. You will come to a point one day where your needs will be your priority again. No doubt. But while you are doing this day-to-day mom job, while they're solely in your care, they'll be a major marker on your happiness barometer.

What Do YOU Want?

The cheerleader in me gets all fired up for striving to achieve whatever *you* define as happiness and success! Remember you're in charge. You are the author of your story. You are the architect of your life.

Know this as well, your definition of happiness and success will probably change many times in your life the same as your expectations. It will most likely be a version of the same core things, but as you add people to your life you see the ripple in the pond that spreads wider and wider as your happiness is connected to those around you.

That is magnified when one of those people is your child.

Here's the thing; unrealistic expectations are a direct route to disappointment and frustration. Parenting can be a much smoother ride for you and your child if you are both clear on your expectations. Make them reasonable and obtainable for both of you.

Kids are people.

They require the same people skills as anyone in your life. It's a good rule of thumb to treat them as well as you would anyone else. Use your same people savvy for cooperation. Be polite and respectful to get consideration and respect back in return.

Be the person you want them to be.

Mommy

Be honorable to be honored.

Those aren't positivity memes for your journal. They are elegantly simple ideals of humanity that matter. You're in charge of raising a human being who will contribute to a world made better by their efforts and yours.

I want to give you everything I can to make this a little easier, a lot more fun, and empower you with reassurance that you already have the big answers inside you and the immeasurable ability to do this job wisely.

I'm going to keep reminding you of that.

Here's one thing I know for sure.

Your child will strive for excellence when you lead by example.

Excellence has no point of completion. Neither does being a mom.

You meet needs. That's what you do.

You will find yours can be met in different ways.

Now you're probably thinking that I'm going to talk about *self-love*. I'm not. Not in those words. I must confess, I don't like that term. It sounds self-centered and anyone who is or has ever been a mom

What Do YOU Want?

knows you can't be focused on yourself when you have one eye on a toddler about to bump their head on the coffee table and the other eye on the dog who's chewing your dining room chairs and the proverbial eyes in the back of your head on a preschooler dumping their graham crackers into the fireplace.

At certain junctures in this job there is no me-time. It will come later. Remember the mantra of *not now doesn't mean not ever*.

Now don't start the expletives under your breath and tell me I'm mommy-shaming you because you wish you had me-time. I wish you did, too. It's not that it's wrong to want it. It's just not practical to expect it.

Thinking that you should be able to carve time for bubble baths and facials will only frustrate you when they don't happen. Sometimes there aren't enough hours in the day or enough hands to help. When you expect to have that time to yourself and it doesn't happen then you end up feeling like you're failing your child and yourself.

I want you to save yourself from that trap. Guilt sends you backward. It's like the *Lose a Turn* space on a *Wheel of Fortune* spin.

Guilt is a huge emotion that will sneak up and try to seize you many times over the course of your mom career.

Mommy

You can't feel good about yourself if you let guilt take over.

When you do this job with every conscious intent to get it done so that your child has what they need to go out into the world you will have the reward of knowing you made that happen. It will be worth the sacrifices.

But why do you feel a certain way about something, but your best friend is the kind of mom who lets the issue slide? Why do you react and overreact about specific issues?

Why does this all feel so hard?

Think about your job description.

Moms answer questions.

Millions of questions.

You are supposed to know things.

Lots of things.

Everything a child can think of to ask.

You explain.

What Do YOU Want?

You describe.

You repeat to get the point across.

They ask again.

You explain again.

You need answers so you'll have them to give. Let's get you some.

CHAPTER 3

Legacy & How to Build One

The statement *it isn't all about you anymore,* is true.

Here's what else is true. It's not ALL about you but it is still about you.

Spoiler alert! There's no way to do this job totally dedicated and not take it personally.

I *want* you to take this job personally.

VERY personally.

Without putting your emotional self on the line, you risk missing the return.

You need all the information you can get about the reasons you feel, react, respond, and believe the way you do. That self-awareness is golden. It's the key to having great relationships including

Mommy

and most importantly of all, the one you have with your child. It will unlock their happiness and yours.

You want the best for your child. You obsess over the best car seat, or the best preschool, or the best soccer cleats, or the best college.

Be your best self. Isn't that what everyone is telling you?

Okay, another overused keyword phrase that has become a cliché I wish would drop from favor. I'm asking you to think of it in a new way.

Be your best self sounds like a noble cause. What's interesting is people use this same line of thought without realizing it when they say *I'm doing my best* as an excuse for not doing all they can do in a situation. Or when they make excuses for others who fall short of expectations by saying, *well, they did the best they could*.

Seriously? The word best is a superlative. We diminish it when we use it as an excuse.

We also minimize it with the idea that it is stagnant or fixed.

Best sounds like an endpoint.

You're always changing and so are your circumstances. There's no such thing as best if you keep doing it. What if Thomas Edison

Legacy & How to Build One

had been satisfied with beautiful hand-made candles for the best lighting or Steve Jobs said a phone that simply made and received calls without wires was the best version of a cell phone? What if Simone Biles declared her double twist was her best and never attempted the triple?

The top is always moving up.

The bar is always rising.

Best is momentary. It's dependent on constant repetitive performance. That's the kicker. The hard part and the reason that best is illusive is because you have to be all in all the time or the ball drops.

I challenge you to think differently. Instead of measuring your performance in terms of reaching your best, strive for excellence. Seek improvement in yourself where the effort sustains quality. Make it an ongoing, ever-evolving process not a target.

This isn't positivity overload. This is setting a worthy goal.

Strive to be excellent.

If you're a fan of the Marvel franchise, then you know Stan Lee the creator had a motto for his superheroes.

Excelsior. The Latin definition is *ever upward*.

Mommy

Upward is a direction not a destination.

You aren't a done deal. Your personal development isn't complete just because your childhood is over and you're a grown-up. There is much to do especially as a mom to keep evolving and grow.

You are a marvelous combination of factors that come together in as many ways as there are people. I put those factors into four basic categories, your legacy, your wiring, your location, and your relationships. All are vital components to the sum of you.

They are like the game of *Jenga*.

The blocks fit together but one piece out of place can cause a weakness in the whole structure. Each one affects the others. One can make the others feel a bit shaky. One can bring the whole down into a pile of rubble.

You are your child's fortress.

Their shelter.

You need a strong foundation and framework. You've got to stand against the storms.

The best defense you have for your own happiness is self-awareness.

Legacy & How to Build One

The best assurance that you can protect your child is to have those tools to pass on to them.

You are their template.

But who are you?

Let's start at the beginning with that part of you that was given to you by those who cared for you and about you. This is your legacy.

Your first instructors were your parents or guardians. They provided the soil where you were planted. They watered you with physical care to one degree or another. Hopefully they fed you with love and affection. Whether you got all three of those key ingredients or didn't shaped the person you are today. The amounts they gave or didn't give were key. All you knew about being a child was provided by their input.

Whether the grownups around you lied or were honest, fought fairly or harmed, coped or copped out, showed up or failed you all made an impact on shaping your *soul stuff*. That core essence of your knowledge about being a human. Those factors became the blueprint you used to build your life. You form relationships based on them. They're also the framework for your parenting style.

You've already thought for a moment about your relationship with your mother when you examined your expectations.

Mommy

Let's talk about all the people in your childhood.

Stay with me here, this isn't going to be a psychoanalysis session. I'm not asking you to try to delve into the deep end of the pathology of your family pool. You get to choose how much you want to dig but know that asking yourself to consider some fact-finding questions will give you access to some incredibly helpful and useful insight.

What this will do is give you some food for thought about how your childhood has shaped your perception of parenthood.

It's about using your experiences by not allowing them to hold you back in any way.

It's also about leaving blame behind so you can move forward faster without carrying so much.

I call that *emotional ergonomics*. Shedding the unnecessary layers makes it so much easier to go further faster. Carry less with you as you go.

If you're fortunate enough to have had a great childhood, then this will be easy. If not, it might be painful to relive but it's the first step in assuring your child has better.

The moment you're born you immediately begin to become you. Some things about you are genetically wired, we'll talk more about

Legacy & How to Build One

the roles of nature and nurture later, but it's very important that you recognize that much of who you are relies on the physical and emotional environment of your early home life. The level of care you received early on or the lack of care has made a difference in how you view yourself and how you react in the world. Care encompasses a wide scope of action.

You had physical needs of course as every child does. Food and shelter are basics. This also includes safety. A child is a vulnerable and defenseless creature. They have no concept of physical danger until they learn by experience or someone teaches them. They depend on adults for protection from anything or anyone that might harm them.

Then there are the matters of the mind and heart. This is what I call *spirit stuff*. Love and affection are the starter seeds for self-esteem, self-confidence, and self-sufficiency. This is the solid ground you stand on when the world tries to shake you.

Then there's what I call the *soul stuff*. This is your moral core. The part of you that discerns right from wrong, good from evil, fair from unjust. This is the part of you that decides the standards you set for what is acceptable in your life. It is also the part of you that accepts or rejects the behavior of others and your own behavior as desirable or undesirable. Those standards are not a preset. You acquire them as you go. The care-giving adults in your life are your example.

Mommy

So, let's look at your legacy.

- Were your parents present in your early life? This is crucial to how you parent. Role models make a difference.

- What roles did gender play? This will directly affect how you deal with either gender child. It will also influence the role you expect to fill and the one you expect of your partner.

- How did you parents relate to each other? This is important for understanding your viewpoint of how your relationship with your partner will work.

- Were they respectful and supportive of each other as partners and as parents? This shapes your parenting style.

- How did your parents relate to you?

- Did they tune in to you emotionally? Was there genuine connection?

- Were your parents emotionally balanced? Okay. No funny stuff here. I know most families have something wacky or quirky about the way they function. I'm talking about anything about your parents that prevented them from being there for you emotionally.

Legacy & How to Build One

- How did your parents manage conflict between each other?

- How did your parents manage conflict with you?

- How were you disciplined?

- How did your parents handle conflict between you and any siblings?

- Did your parents make an effort to instruct you on how to manage conflict?

- Did your parents set an example for problem-solving?

- Did you parents have healthy coping skills?

- How did they respond to your responses to conflict or difficulty?

- Were you rewarded or punished for your efforts?

- Did your parents use physical punishment?

- What was their punishment method?

- Were they mindful of their words?

- Did they draw a line between constructive criticism and shame?

Mommy

- Did they emphasize character development and value integrity, honesty, empathy, compassion, and service?

- Was respect expected and given?

My husband has always been an entrepreneur. That means he has a great deal of experience in being a boss. He has a philosophy that rather than not wanting to understand certain concepts, folks often don't have the tools to discern and make decisions.

All you know is what you know.

Think about the simplicity of that philosophy. Your ability to do something and the quality of your performance is based on your knowledge, not your intelligence alone.

You need information.

You have to learn in order to do.

You learned things early in your development. That information was provided by your environment and the people around you. That's your legacy.

Here's something I want you to get down deep inside.

Legacy & How to Build One

The lasting effects of your legacy are not etched in stone. They're not even written in Sharpie permanent marker. It was what it was, but you can change the impact.

You control the result.

You can stop the fallout. That means you can continue the good parts of your legacy and break the cycle of any part of it you feel needs to change.

You come into motherhood with a skill set, full or lacking that someone else provided for you. Now you get to look at it and see what you want to repeat and what you want to take out of the picture and what you need to add for your child and your mothering experience.

If you choose to recognize the deficits instead of lamenting them, you can use them as power tools.

You're in charge of this show.

You get to set the ground rules and the requirements.

You get to do it YOUR way.

Doesn't that sound divine?

Mommy

You're the mom boss and this is your domain.

Let's stop here and take a moment to celebrate that.

YAASS!!!!! Yay, you Mommy!

CHAPTER 4

Wiring & Why It Matters

Next let's talk about your "wiring". This is the part of you that is your personality and temperament. You may be thinking, *aren't those the same thing?* Think of it this way. Personality type indicates *what* you're inclined to do, and temperament is *how* you do it.

Why do I want you to think about this? Because these are vital components in not only you as a person, but you as a mom. Understanding this part of you opens you to so much insight into why you choose to handle things in the way you do. It identifies your emotional style.

That emotional style is the core of your mom style.

Here's a simile for you to get a visual. Your personality is like the electrical wiring in a building. For all of the systems to work power must be supplied. A network of wiring is set in place to get the power where it needs to go. There are several different patterns for that path to take and that get the job done. Think of your personality as your power source for your behavior. Your temperament is the pathway.

Think of all the adjectives you use to describe yourself and others. You say optimistic, pessimistic, shy, gregarious, impulsive, cautious, generous, stingy, compassionate, and indifferent. Think of the nouns you use as descriptors like leader, follower, peacemaker, instigator, go-getter, and procrastinator.

What are those ingredients that make up a person's personality? Where do they come from? Experts argue this all the time.

You recognize that dry wit you have like your dad or that same moodiness as your brother. You may be a screamer when angry like your mother or hypersensitive to criticism like your grandmother. Whether that's genetic or a result of mirroring their behavior, the result is those emotions are the catalysts for your behavior.

Why does that matter for this conversation we're having about being a mom? Emotions set off a chain reaction that leads to how you act and react. Your child is on the receiving end of that result most of the time. In fact, they are usually part of whatever sets you off emotionally. Emotions ignite behavior. What you do when the emotions of the moment hit will influence your child's emotional style, set an example for behavior and the pattern repeats.

Wiring & Why It Matters

See that connection? You are shaping your child's emotional style with yours.

Remember not all of your emotions are undesirable. There are wonderful emotions you have every day as well that you want to pass on to your child. Emotions can be fabulous. Those are the ones you're always seeking. The ones that make it all worthwhile.

So, let's talk about some questions to ask yourself about your wiring.

- What are the personality traits you admire about yourself? Brag, boast, show some swagger.

- Which of your personality traits do other people admire about you? Own your fabulosity.

- What traits do you admire in others?

- Do you view those traits you admire as favorable for your life? You don't have to figure it out if you see what works. It's like painting by numbers. or having the answers guide to the crossword puzzle. Learn from the successes of others.

- Which of your personality traits do you wish were different? Honesty is key. List but don't beat yourself up here.

Mommy

- Can you imagine them changed?

- What can you do to make those changes?

- Are you willing to make those changes?

Now you might be thinking *Becki, I don't need this task. Change is hard and I'm tired.*

I get it. I really do. But here's what I know about being a mom. There will never be a time you question yourself, doubt yourself, or find more fault with yourself. Every day you will look at your child and assess yourself.

I don't want you to waste emotional energy. That's the energy that is made of your physical and emotional stamina, your coping skills, your resilience and resourcefulness to get the job done. I want you to conserve those and store them in reserve for when you need them most.

Emotions naturally move close to the surface when you become a parent. That doesn't mean you can't control them or are powerless when they occur. Don't settle for the default setting if it doesn't work in your favor.

The beauty of self-awareness is you can use these attributes to become who you want to be. You can build on them or recognize the need for change. You may be quick to anger or hard to rattle. You may be carefree or a worrier, a night owl or an early bird, an adrenaline junkie or a scaredy cat, Pollyanna or a Chicken Little. These things aren't permanent if you desire them to change.

> *Change that begins with self-awareness is ALWAYS possible.*

You can set the standard for what is acceptable behavior in your home by controlling your emotional style and instructing and insisting you child do the same. This will go a long way in helping your child learn to manage their emotions and their behavior.

You don't always get to do what you feel.

You must learn to control those impulses. It's best to learn that early in life. That's your job as a mom, teaching your child impulse control and personal responsibility.

It's never too early to instruct good coping.

Managing your emotions is an essential coping skill.

But where do you start?

To begin to change and take charge of your emotions use a very simple alteration in your language. Remember words are a power source.

Haven't you said in response to someone in a conflict, *how do you think that makes me feel? Do you know how mad you made me?* You've given away your power. You've put that person or that situation in control of your emotions.

Start a change today. Instead of saying *it makes me feel,* or *you made me feel,* say *I feel.*

I feel really angry is a statement of your choice.

See the difference? In the first statement the emotion is in charge directing you. In the second you are in control of your feelings. You're in charge. That positions you for success.

Sometimes change begins with a simple awareness and requires only a slight tweak. Sometimes it requires a major shift in thinking. Demonstrate the power of excellence. Plant the concept firmly in their mind that excellence is the path to finding their definition of happiness and success. You can make adjustments. Think of it as a short in your power source. You need to locate the cause and repair it. You may find that it's time for a system upgrade. Rewiring is always an option.

Whether the components come to you preprogrammed genetically

Wiring & Why It Matters

or by imitation is an age-old question. Does it really matter? Yes, because you have complete control of your young child's environment. You set the stage. They watch you for cues. The environment part is totally you.

Children are like mirrors. They reflect what is in front of them.

You hear yourself asking *why are they acting like this?* If you don't like the behavior your child is choosing, then look at your own for clues.

What they see they do.

As their parent, that can be a heavy burden of responsibility.

Or it can be a call to action.

Be your excellent self. You won't always hit your mark, but you'll be closer.

Think long-term. You can do anything for a moment that will reap lasting results.

Think upgrade.

It's also a fabulous opportunity for you to give them an amazing start in life.

CHAPTER 5

Location & What it Means

I hear you saying, Becki what does where I live have to with anything? That's not the location I'm talking about. I use this term to describe where you are in your life in terms of your career, relationships, financial position, age, and experiences.

This is phase of life stuff.

Many times, age isn't as big a factor as the others because women no longer follow a traditional pattern. Neither do men. Times have changed. Marriage comes later if at all. Careers often delay motherhood. Some women and men find a permanent partner before adding a baby to their lives while others choose to go it alone.

Sometimes biology plays a part in the timing. Infertility issues, adoption processes, personal preferences all contribute to when you choose motherhood. Motherhood is more a choice now than ever before.

Mommy

Your life history, your experiences, and where you've been on the road of life so far is important because it can be an indicator for your preparedness for this job.

Think of determining your location as writing your resume.

What qualifications do you bring to this job?

What are your skills and experiences?

Good news or unsettling, this may be the only job that requires no previous experience in it. You won't hear anyone say *you don't have enough experience to be considered a mom at this time.*

You get this job first time out of the gate.

No trial-period.

No test-drive.

You create your qualifications as you go.

It's on the job training.

But you do have other experiences you might not have thought about that you can use for this job. Let's talk about that.

Location & What it Means

- Take a moment to think about all the accomplishments you've had in any area of your life. The academic and career milestones are easy to spot. Remember to include the successful friendships, family relationships, and community service. You already have a lot of human relations experience.

- Think of the struggles you've overcome. Not in a ruminating way but as a sense of pride at your resourcefulness and survival skills. These are the same ones you'll need now.

- Think of the adventures you've lived. You've probably done some pretty cool stuff. Some things were great learning experiences.

- Remember all the heartache you've survived. This is where the power of resilience comes in.

- Consider the risks you've taken. Some you saw coming and some you didn't. Some were acts of bravery.

- Recall the mistakes you've made. I call these acts of elimination because after you make one you usually try hard not to repeat.

- Recall the missteps you've made. These were near misses that didn't go as badly as a mistake might have but still required a degree of recovery on your part.

- Do you see a pattern in the missteps and mistakes you've made?

Mommy

- Recount the lessons you've learned.

Your location currently is the mom road. You have other markers that define where you are in your life that have to do with your career, your relationships, and your goals. But the mommy marker is the pin on the map that means the most because it requires so much of your time and energy. It affects everything else.

It's the 24/7 of you and the rest is noise by comparison.

That's not to minimize the juggling act you're required to perform. You have a partner, boss, friends, family, and assorted other variables to deal with along the way.

Because this is a lifetime job - let's call it being Mom Emeritus of this mommy career, then you will be a mom at different stages of not only your child's life but your own. You start out younger and you age as you go. Your financial status probably changes. Your relationships with others change. Your life desires and goals change. You have many more experiences. That means you learn as you go, and you adapt.

What does that mean for you as a mom?

Let's keep using the road analogy. You pack everything and set out with a destination – to get your child safely into and out into the

Location & What it Means

world equipped with everything they'll need. You set your GPS to that place you describe as happiness and success and begin.

There's the road itself. The road conditions change with the landscape. There are the little bumps you roll over and the potholes you don't see that jar you when you hit them. There are the unexpected detours that cause you to veer away from your original path and you find yourself going on an unknown back road. Something might happen to cause you to careen over a cliff.

The visibility will fluctuate with the weather. Some periods are sunny and clear, and you may even be able to enable your cruise control and enjoy the scenery. Then others are cloudy, and it feels gray and endless. You navigate storms that hit from nowhere and those you see coming and you grip the steering wheel so hard you think your hands will never unclench.

The fog of confusion can descend on you when a difficulty sets in, and you have to trust that the road is there though you may not be able to see it through that fog more than a few feet at time. By continuing forward, you are still headed toward your original destination. It hasn't moved because your visibility is limited.

Then there are mountains to decide whether to go through or around, hills, valleys, deserts, plains, woods, and swamps. All manner of terrain and topography along the way will provide your landscape view. You may find it hard to believe in a difficult moment,

Mommy

but there is something beautiful along the way every mile you go. Have you ever seen a dust storm? The way they roll over a horizon is like billowing topaz fabric unfolding. Lightening is scary but it is quite magical in its display. Rain can be depressing but have you ever watched the drops as they hit a window or a windshield? They literally dance in unison.

See, what I mean?

It's all about the lens you choose as to what you'll see.

Everything in life is viewed by you by some measurement. Good or bad, negative or positive, favorable or unfavorable you qualify everything in your life in some way. It's how you make decisions. Your personality wiring may tend toward the negative but remember you can steer it any direction with intent.

You've read all the recent mental health data about brain chemistry and you know that the brain uses your thoughts as fuel.

It's mood food.

You buy acai bowls, protein shakes, raw juices, and smoothies that would make a rabbit jealous. Think of your thought diet with the same focus.

Location & What it Means

Remember, your brain never stops thinking. You're constantly feeding it. You control the input to get the output you desire.

I know this sounds like a lot of effort and you're thinking you don't need any more to do. My point is you are going to be having thoughts anyway because in order to keep you alive your brain works non-stop. No way around that. Doesn't it make sense to choose your thoughts since you have the ability? To regulate them for your health?

You know worry, stress, and anxiety have detrimental effects on your body. That's why meditation, yoga, and deep breathing work so well. They focus your thoughts. They move them.

We're going to talk about taking charge in all areas of your life.

The first place you can begin is your thoughts.

Your thoughts produce your feelings. Those emotions give instructions back to your brain and you act on them with your behavior. This is what behavior modification is all about. It's the modality used for quitting smoking, overeating, and anxiety as well as many other issues.

Change your thoughts to change your behavior.

Mommy

Change your thoughts to change your life.

You know this works.

You've used gratitude to replace feeling hopeless.

You've used positivity to replace negativity.

You're going to think. Don't you want it to feel good? To be content?

Think of your current location as your starting line. Wherever you are on your road, choose where you want to be and set your thoughts like coordinates on the map. You're driving. You get to pick the destination.

CHAPTER 6

Relationships & How They Work

It's easy to get so focused on being a mom that you think that's the only relationship you have. It sucks your energy.

Because you live in this world you have lots of relationships. They vary in significance and intensity. The differences are what can make relationships interesting and worthwhile and or difficult.

Think about what we've talked about so far.

Your legacy is the learned behavior template for what you know about how relationships work or don't work and what is acceptable behavior from others and for yourself.

Your wiring shapes your emotional responses in relationships in terms of your personality, your temperament, and your likes and dislikes.

Your experiences lay the groundwork for expectations and repeated patterns. History matters.

Your life location determines who else is involved.

You're probably thinking in terms of your family, your friends and your partner as your relationships. In actuality the scope is much broader. Take a moment and think of all the people you come into contact within a day. Have you ever considered these are also relationships in your life?

You have to interact with other people on a daily basis. Why does this matter?

Healthy relationships are vital to your happiness. Learning how to be successful in relationships is crucial for teaching your child how to be part of a community. It's the beginning of good citizenship. You're their role model for relationship-building, conflict management, and best problem-solving practices.

To take a look at how those affect your mom role, I break them into groups by frequency and importance or necessity in your life.

Let's look at those groups. Start with a wide view. I call this your

Relationships & How They Work

periphery. From others at your gym, to the sales associates in the stores where you shop, the tellers at the bank, the barista at the coffee shop on the corner, the clerk at the post office, your neighbors, members of your church, the people who walk their dog at the same park.

Your child watches you for cues of how to treat others. Ask yourself a few questions about these relationships.

- Are you mindful of how you treat other people even those you don't know but encounter in your day?

- Are you mindful of how you treat others whose services you rely on or use in your daily life?

- Are you polite and respectful in your tone?

- Do you insist your child is respectful to others no matter the relationship?

- Do you voice your dissatisfaction or frustration with people easily?

Move in a bit and you'll see you have people in your life that are there by *association*. What does that mean? These people are part of the life of someone or something you choose to have in yours.

Mommy

They come with the territory so to speak. You have a job, so you have co-workers and a boss. Your friends have other friends and partners that they bring into the mix. Your partner comes into your relationship with friends and family of their own. People in that family marry or form partnerships in other families and the circle widens.

Being a mom brings a set of people into your life that you wouldn't have otherwise. Teachers are an example. Your child has classmates and friends. Those friends have parents you interact with as a result and so on.

When those relationships come into play in your life ask yourself these questions.

- Are you accepting of those people who come into your life by association?

- Do you put the people you care about in the middle of any disagreement you have with someone they bring into your relationship?

- Do you consider the person you care for when you draw boundaries for others in their life?

- Do you make the person you care for choose between you and others in their life?

Relationships & How They Work

- Are you disrespectful when you talk about these people in front of your child?

- Do you compromise when someone by association causes a problem between you and the person you care about in order to keep the peace?

Now, move your view in more and you'll see you have a number of *chosen* relationships. These are the ones that you have sought out and nurtured over time and with considerable effort. They are reciprocal and mutual commitments.

Your child learns so much by watching the way your friendships work.

They hear what you say and model what they see. Ask yourself these questions.

- Do you value and give respect and loyalty in your friendships?

- Do you keep the confidence of your friends or do you tell things you shouldn't?

- Are you honest in your friendships?

Mommy

- Do you say uncomplimentary or derogatory things about your friends?

- Do you voice your frustration or displeasure when you become angry with a friend?

- Are you happy for your friends and refrain from jealousy?

- Do you give of your time to your friends freely or begrudgingly?

- Do you openly complain when your friends need your time and attention?

Then there's your family circle. This is your parents or guardians, your siblings, grandparents and assorted other members. These are the opportunities you have for deep emotional enrichment with the people you love where respect is expected and given in reciprocal and loyalty is valued.

How you interact with all of the players is vital to your emotional well-being and your child's. Like all other aspects of their development, they learn from your example. Think about how you are presenting those relationships to them. It will affect how they interact with those important people and receive value from that.

You may be required to move past your own feelings or adjust your

Relationships & How They Work

attitude or even forgive a family member in order to provide your child with the family they deserve. You may have to tolerate your brother or sister or move past the resentment you feel about your dad or curb your frustration with your mom.

Resist calling them out and call a truce instead.

Your story with them is your story.

Your child deserves to make their own history.

Without carrying your baggage.

I know this is HARD.

Remember you child trusts you to tell them the truth. They believe you have their interests at heart. If you hamper or encumber their relationship or deny them access to family members you are robbing them of experiences that are owed to them.

Family is a birthright not something you earn. Your family belongs to your child. Unless there is a possibility of your child being in danger, give them that.

If the situation is the opposite and a family member chooses not to be in your child's life, no matter the reason, you must do everything you can to make your child feel it's that member who is on the deficit side of the ledger.

They are losing out on the wonderfulness of your child.

Then there's the relationship you have with the romantic love of your life. I always tell people this is the gamble of a lifetime. Even if you don't see yourself as a risk-taker you enter a romantic relationship fully vulnerable and open with the possibility for it to go either way.

You're as emotionally exposed as is humanly possible and you wager your well-being that the person you have chosen will protect you and never exploit you or your commitment to them. When a child is involved, those possibilities and their impact pervade their life as well.

Hopefully, this is a permanent relationship your child can count on for stability and continuity. This is where your child first learns how a love commitment works. It is imperative that you provide them with the healthiest example.

- How do you and your partner demonstrate your affection for each other?

Relationships & How They Work

- How do you demonstrate your frustration or disappointment with each other?

- Do you both fight fairly?

- Do you have the same conflict styles?

- Are you careful to not include your child in the conflict?

- Do you refrain from criticizing your partner in front of your child?

- Do you make it clear what is acceptable and unacceptable in your relationship in an age-appropriate way to your child?

- How do you support each other when the frustrations come from outside your relationship?

- Does your child realize they are not responsible for the quality of your relationship with you partner?

- Are you working together to raise your child?

- Are your goals and levels of commitment the same?

- Can your child count on your solidarity as a couple to support them?

Mommy

I implore you to give this your full attention. I see so many parents conduct their relationship as if they are the only two people involved. If only this were true, much heartache and devastation would be avoided.

You think you're punishing your only partner for their misconduct.

You think you're exacting revenge only on them for their indiscretion.

You think they are the only ones you hurt with your words or your indifference, or your rage.

You believe they are the only ones you cheat on and betray.

If only that were true.

I wish that was true.

My heart has broken more times than I can recount over the devastation parents have heaped upon their children. Those little shoulders were never intended to hold grown-up burdens. It is almost inconceivable to me that adults can bring these unassuming creatures into the world and subject them to emotional annihilation.

Relationships & How They Work

Soul-crushing should be a punishable crime.

Be judicious with your knowledge.

Children don't need to know the intimate details of your relationship with your partner.

Grown-ups have grown-up problems.

Kids are not grown-ups.

There should be a time in a child's life when they are not subject to the harsh realities. It is your job as their mom to protect them in a healthy way with age-appropriate concepts and language.

Remember that the relationship you have with your partner is inseparable from your child's relationship with both of you.

That one becomes three relationships at risk.

You're making decisions that will affect your child without their input or permission. They have no control at all. Don't you hate it when you feel you have no control over situations important to you? This is THEIR life you are messing with as you act and react.

Mommy

Never lose sight of the fact that you are preserving or disturbing their way of life.

It's also your mandate to give your child the tools to choose their own partner wisely in the future. Will they want to replicate what they learned by your relationship or will they know what to avoid? Think about your behavior, your language, your coping skill level, your resiliency, and your ability or inability to control your temper and moderate your emotions.

Think of your deal breakers and your standards for what you deem acceptable and unacceptable from your partner. Your child is watching and learning. They will imitate.

Think of teaching them about how to be in a love relationship as if you were designing a love relationship for them. The one you hope they'll have one day.

Model the relationship you wish for them.

If your current partner is not your child's parent, then use the same guidelines for that relationship. There are so many facets to blended family dynamics.

The main theme should be preserving your child's relationships with the important people in their lives.

Relationships & How They Work

The more love your child has the better.

Make sure everyone is living up to their obligation for that purpose.

If you bring someone new into your life as a partner, then remember that they are also in your child's life by association. Make sure they have your child's best interests at heart. Put your child first. Ask that of everyone. Then no matter the situation or the players, you've got your child covered.

Now, let's talk about the relationship that brought you to this book.

Experts will tell you that no one can make you happy but you. I'm here to tell you ultimately you make the decision whether to allow others to determine it, of course. I will also tell you that unless you stay very vigilant with your emotions, others can be the source of much discontent in your relationships.

You spend your life pursuing, cultivating, nurturing and maintaining relationships from the casual to the lifelong. Relationships are about interpersonal interactions. It's a part of the love and belonging need in all of us.

It's like that on steroids where your children are concerned.

You've probably heard the saying that you're only as happy as your unhappiest child. They can be a barometer of your contentment for sure. Afterall, they are your heart and soul, and their care is your job.

To try to separate your happiness from theirs is nearly impossible. I have tried it myself but am unable to do so completely. So, there. I said it.

Parenting is a relationship. It's easy to forget you must take the same sort of steps to fulfill your part as you do with the other relationships in your life. The same rules for success apply. Respect, trust, courtesy, honesty, and dependability are required in the same way for both of you to be fulfilled.

It's easy to slack off and think your child knows you care. So why do all those little things?

The one that is the easiest to let slide is courtesy. This is all about those things that make and keep life pleasant. The little kindnesses and politeness we use for civility. Doesn't your child deserve the same thoughtfulness you demonstrate to other people outside your home? Isn't it wonderful to be spoken to in a warm tone and to receive the respect of manners? Give it to receive it then make it non-negotiable. Don't you want a home where everyone treats each other well and there is an atmosphere of cooperation and kindness? Think of the amount of stress this relieves.

Respect. That's another relationship tool that is easily lost. Intimacy

Relationships & How They Work

that comes from living in the same house, sharing the same experiences, and the familiarity of habits and shared rituals often leads to a shortage of mutual respect.

It's easy to forget the civil niceties in the nitty-gritty of everyday life.

Your mom-child relationship is unique and unlike any other in its intensity and depth of devotion. But like the other relationships in your life, it needs attention and vigilance.

If you let your friendships become routine, they can lose their meaningfulness. If you allow your family relationships to go unattended, they will diminish in their closeness.

You know what effort it takes to maintain a great marriage or partnership, so why shouldn't you be prepared to do the same for your relationship with your child?

Don't take it for granted.

Don't assume it will be fine simply because it's expected.

Right now, in this moment, make this relationship what you want it to be. Remember, you lay the groundwork.

You're prepping the soil of this child's beginning.

Mommy

You are providing the nourishment and the nurturing.

Dandelions or orchids.

This garden is yours.

CHAPTER 7

Who ARE You?

You'll be many things in your life and those will be determined to a great degree by the people in your life. The trick is to fulfill those roles without relinquishing the essence of you in the process. No time is this more difficult than being a mom to a young child.

Because you give of yourself for their care you must be careful not to give up your core identity. You don't have to do that to be a great mom. As a role model, it's most desirable to show how you can be a part of someone's story and remain an individual. That example says to your child that they will be happier if they maintain their sense of self in all relationships.

We've talked about making constructive changes in your goals and your expectations and even in your temperament style. There are life desires you will put on hold while you do your mom job. Keep that mantra of *not now doesn't mean not ever* in your mind. Even in those times that anything other than the present moment seems unthinkable or at least very far away from now.

Mommy

With the many moving parts of motherhood, things will feel out of control at times.

Out of control and unchangeable are two different things.

You can't change the fact that your baby doesn't sleep through the night or your toddler has speech issues, or your grader schooler wets the bed, or your teen is painfully shy. Those situations have been presented to you. But you control how you respond.

I hear you. You're saying, *Yeah Becki I hear that all the time, but I can't help how I feel.*

Now, I'm going to tell you I hear *that* all the time.

Let me ask you something. Have you ever been really sad, and you watched a funny movie and your mood changed? Have you ever whispered *calm down* to yourself when you were angry? Have you ever stopped yourself before you said something that was going to cause a disagreement or hurt feelings? How about telling yourself you can do this one more time when your body and your mind say no. Then see, you can control how you respond when unfavorable emotions hit your mind.

Have you ever been in traffic and taken an alternative route to make an appointment on time? Have you ever had a coworker fail to perform on a project and you picked up the slack and saved the

Who ARE You?

day? You were confronted with a problem and made a decision to handle it. You couldn't make the traffic go away or force the coworker to do their job, but you could respond in a constructive way.

Those seem obvious and reasonable, right? You always have choices. They might not be the ones you want to have as options. Remember you may not get to choose *what is,* but you can take charge of *what now*.

That's a very powerful point to hold onto. In the fog of confusion that comes over you in difficult times you can use it as headlights on the unknown road or a flashlight in the dark tunnel or hallway to see your way through.

New Mom You

Early on in your mom job in your efforts to do a great job, you may be too open to suggestion and think everyone knows better than you in a difficulty.

Let me say here your truest guide is your gut.

Therein lies the inner sanctum of innate wisdom.

That's a fancy way to say intuition which is a way to say that part of

Mommy

you that knows that you know without knowing why. You simply feel it.

It is there to serve you if you let it.

What does this have to do with your identity?

You will never question your belief system, your knowledge, your family legacy, your abilities, your sanity, as much or as often as you will as a mother. Let's face it. Someone or multiple people are looking to you for answers. They're expecting you to give them direction. They're counting on you to be there or to always show up.

Here's what I want you to grasp. That part of you that is your moral core, your essence will remain no matter the circumstance.

But nothing will alter your self-image more than being a mom because someone depending on you is always judging your performance.

You are always judging you.

Your self-view will change because of what is required of you at each age and stage and phase of your child's life. You will morph at times to meet their needs. Some days you might wonder what happened to that girl you were before all this wonderful chaos came into your life.

Who ARE You?

The shear physical engagement it takes to be a new mom is truly astounding. Quite frankly, it can be a shock to the system. Your sleep patterns are unquestionably the most disrupted. Your diet and meal schedule are now catch a bite when you can and try not to eat in what I call the "one for you one for me" pattern. You find that even bland baby food and teething biscuits are appealing when you're hungry enough or too exhausted to prepare anything else for yourself. You probably take shortcuts with your hygiene, your social interactions and the way you connect with your partner.

You feel like a shell of the former you.

Or you may not recognize yourself at all.

May I suggest that what you see is the raw you. The part that is there when all the other stuff is cleared away. Here's your chance to not be "on" all the time, to not be playing any part other than the one right in front of you.

Your baby or small child appreciates the real you in a way no one else will ever do. That unabashed love you feel for them comes right back to you. What they offer you is as real as it gets. Enjoy it. It won't change but it's proximity will. We'll talk about that later.

You may find you don't have as much time for your friends or if they don't have kids, they may not get what you're going through or identify with your feelings. Cut them some slack. You know you didn't get it either before you had this job. You're still the same person in your core. It's simply that you are less concerned with certain things and hyper-focused on others.

Then take a moment to remember that your childless friends are still the exact same people as well. The ones you were attracted to because they were smart, funny, loyal, interesting, told the best stories or get your jokes like nobody else. Whatever brought them into your world will change only if you let it.

Sometimes you will grow apart from others who don't share your location in life and that's okay.

Your focus has changed now that you're a mom so what you're looking for in a friend may change as well. This is truth of the adage *people coming into your life for a reason, but it may be only for a season*. You know there have been people in your life that meant something to you, and they are no longer a part of it. You have the choice to reach out or not.

Let's talk about you and your partner. The changes are not only to your everyday routine of life but the rhythm of your relationship as well. If you are lucky, the most important person in your life in this mom journey is your partner. This is the person who signed up for this with you. Most everything about that relationship has changed except the original core premise. This is the person you chose to walk the path of life with you through thick and thin,

Who ARE You?

good and bad, health and sickness, money or broke. Now you've thrown another variable into the equation.

Here's what you thought would happen before you had a child.

YOU + PARTNER + BABY = HAPPY LIFE

Remember that?

How do you make sure the equation works out? There are many unknowns that come into play. So, first off let's concentrate on what you do know for sure. The two of you share a chemistry that resulted in this child. Hopefully you have dreams in common for the future and hopes for a life you want to build together.

Look at what else you share now. There are the same trials of interrupted sleep, walking the floors, wiping runny noses, stinky diapers, and baby food- stained clothes. It's like you're soldiers in the same squad.

And you share the giggles and the pride and the wonder before you. This is teamwork at its finest. Approach it that way.

Be a good team player and demand the same of your teammate.

Work hard and play fair.

Mommy

Expect cooperation and give it.

Give props when they're due.

If you don't currently feel like the team is measuring up, then make changes.

Make your needs known.

Be sensitive to your partner's needs in return.

Remember to give feedback in the "sandwich method". That means criticism is always better received between two affirmations. No one likes to be berated so focusing on a genuine positive first makes a person open to hearing what you are trying to convey that they might not want to receive. That's not manipulation or playing mind games to get what you want. It's simply fair rules of engagement without malice. It's about intention. Always.

Don't you want to make it better more than you want to be right?

Then there's the issue of working moms. You chuckle when you hear this absurd phrase come out of someone's mouth or read it in print. Like you're not working?

Who ARE You?

I simply shake my head. Then I get a little indignant, I confess.

What a complete misconception and misnomer. There couldn't be an idea further from the reality.

Being a mom = working full-time.
PERIOD.

Mom is a job position. It's a life-long career. Physical locations may be different, but the job responsibilities remain.

You might say stay-at-home mom but even that's not completely correct. Unless you have a newborn, chances are you are in the road as much or more than you're at your home. Carpool, playdates, lessons of every type, practices, mothers-morning-out, sporting events, and school events means you are too busy to sit at home all day.

You may say work-from-home mom when you describe yourself indicating you have an additional job that you perform alongside your mom job and you do it from a command station in your home whether it's a desk or the dining room table. As an entrepreneur, I've done it from my car! You're required to be good at compartmentalizing those jobs and the tasks for each.

If you say working mom then this is the alternate reality you're

Mommy

describing. I wish we could change that verbiage. If you have an additional job that requires you to leave your home and some of the daily care of your child to someone else, then you say you work.

What about the hours you are in a separate location, but your attention is on what your child needs from you later that day, or the hours of the day and night you are with your child when you're doing all of your mom things for them?

It's ALL work.

I have racked my brain trying to come up with more relatable and adequately descriptive titles for what you do. It's lightening in a bottle. What you do may well be past description in any really all-encompassing way. Unfortunately, the only descriptor that applies is you can have a paid job and your unpaid job. But the benefits with your unpaid mom job can't be tallied or defined.

Don't limit yourself by work location.

Don't define your worth by compensation.

Don't let anyone else do that either.

Likewise, don't allow yourself or anybody to minimize what you do with any sort of definer or label.

Who ARE You?

Ever.

How do you maintain your identity in the process? This is a hard one because it depends on your self-view which by definition only you know, and you determine.

I hear you saying, *I used to be so confident. What happened?*

What is certain is that motherhood will be the catalyst for more self-doubt than any other aspect of life. Why is that? Because there's someone else by whose measure you will always be accountable. You will be tempted to yearn for the validation of other people. It's such a fabulous feeling when someone tells you what a great mom you are. It can also be devastating if you don't receive that sort of feedback.

Your child's life will always be a reflection of what part you played in it and it will be on display daily. Their accomplishments will feel like yours and their missteps will provide you with lots of guilt. You put yourself out there for judgement, like it or not. But here's the good news. You get to judge whether or not someone's opinion matters to you.

You experience change when you become a mom and the changes continue as your child grows.

Let me ask you some questions.

Mommy

- Have you allowed the changes that have happened take you by surprise?

- Are you allowing that surprise to overtake you emotionally?

- Can you see that many of the changes are situational and temporary?

- What part of the change can you lean into and what can you work on?

- Have you considered the ways your friendships have changed?

- Are those changes part of the natural process by design or due to your choice?

- Do you see that you have choices even when you feel like you are no longer in control of many things now in your life?

Listen, this is heaven when it goes well and hell when it doesn't.

You are still here.

This out-of-body thing you're feeling is temporary.

This separation you may feel that has happened between you and the rest of the world will balance out.

Who ARE You?

The romantic chemistry with your partner is not lost forever.

You won't always feel like taking a shower is an act worthy of acclaim.

Your identity won't be defined by your hook-up line number forever.

Your core remains.

Your lifestyle has changed but so has the rewards. If you don't recognize yourself at times, remember you're the same in many ways and in many ways, you are also an *improved* version of that wonderful you. Look for and embrace those changes.

You will amaze yourself with how much you have learned,

How adaptable you have become.

How resourceful you can be.

How strong your body is.

How forgiving you are.

How powerful your spirit is.

Mommy

How fierce you can be.

How huge your heart has become to hold all this love.

Remember that next time you look in the mirror and wonder who's looking back. The same fabulous you is there even when you feel distant from her.

Been There Done That Mom

If you're well into this mom job, then you have enough experience to know the pitfalls and enough knowledge to know it is part wisdom and part trial and error to find what works for you and your child. You also know that many times that wisdom, though rooted in truth, has to be adjusted with each individual child.

You've had more time to make adjustments and more reasons to do so. You may have moved far from the person you used to be in many ways.

- What lifestyle changes have you made?

- How do you feel about them?

- What about you has changed?

Who ARE You?

- How do you feel about the changes in you?

- Name the emotions.

- Do you feel the changes have enhanced your life?

- In what ways have they caused difficulties?

- How have your relationships changed?

- How has your relationship with your partner changed?

- Do you see that some of these changes are situational and will change again as your child grows?

- What are you doing to make the changes work for you?

Whatever age your child is or what complication may be in your life, this time will pass as time always does. While you're waiting to get back to some semblance of life before your child turned it all around know that what will come is a different life made better by what you are doing and who you are.

You'll be different.

That can be a very good thing.

Mommy

Think about how different you are now from the kid you were when you left for college. How different you are from that first day on the job as you started your career. How different you are from the single person who became part of a couple.

Think of your first days as a mom and where you are now. Then close your eyes and think about all the great stuff ahead!

CHAPTER 8

Mommy Missions, Mantras, & Mandates

I am a HUGE believer in the necessity of having a plan in place for anything you do. As I help people through situations and especially difficulties, I always ask them to make a plan of action. This is how you put yourself in the driver's seat of your life.

It's the main ingredient of having control over what happens to you.

It's the blueprint of the life you're building for yourself.

It's the instruction sheet of what to do next.

It's the satellite positioning for getting to where you want to go.

Mommy

See all the ways it influences your life?

Getting clear on what you are willing to do, to change, to accept, to tolerate, to strive for, to let go, to pursue, to believe, to expect, to give up, and to ask for forms your definition of happiness and success.

Believe it or not, not everyone wants what you want.

Everybody has their own definition of what will make them happy. So much frustration comes from not getting clarity on what that is.

Much disappointment also comes from not having a plan in place. That takes thought and consideration of not only what you want to happen but what can happen along the way.

Don't be sidetracked by the element of surprise.

See it coming.

Get clear in your mind how you intend to parent.

Stake your claim.

Do it for your child.

Do it for yourself.

Mommy Missions, Mantras, & Mandates

Your commitment to serving your child's interests must be unwavering.

Now that you've decided what your expectations are, use them as your guide for this next step. We'll talk about the crucial importance of having a plan of action when problem solving in more detail later. Right now, think about this. You have a child's life in your hands. Their emotional development depends on you.

You need a mission statement, an agenda, a mantra, a credo for your intent as a mom. This is for no one else's eyes or ears but yours. You don't need to have it inscribed on a wall hanging for your home or make a vision board or share it on social media.

It can be a mandate in your mind.

Or write across the sky if that's your style.

*This is **your** statement of **your** mission to do **your** way.*

Having that clarity established will carry you through any confusion or doubt you will encounter along the way. It will also help you make your case whenever you're challenged by anyone not on board with your ideals. You'll meet resistance and receive criticism from your mother, your mother-in-law, your spouse or partner, your friends, and sometimes other mothers. It happens.

Mommy

Most importantly it will reset you in the moments that your guard is down, and your anxiety is up. When you need that certainty most, having a clear vision is key.

Clarity anywhere you can find it is golden.

So, take a moment to state your intent as a parent. It can be general, or it can be specific. Wherever you are in this journey may determine how detailed you'll get with this exercise. Your experiences color your view and influence your desires.

Okay, I get it. You might be someone for whom this is a breeze. You have no trouble forming this in your mind and articulating it.

But you're asking where do you start if you just became a mom or if you are already so into the process that it seems too complicated to narrow to a single statement? I get it. This can sound like one of those broad metaphysical questions of life.

What's your purpose?

What's your passion?

What makes you happy?

What's the meaning of life?

Mommy Missions, Mantras, & Mandates

And my personal favorite, wait for it.

Where do you see yourself in five years?

Five years are you kidding me?

I'm sure you don't always know what day of the week it is and many days you can't remember what you had for lunch much less have any idea what the next five years will bring. You probably don't have the time or the patience for philosophical ponderings.

As you consider what you want as you make your mom plan you will see the answers to those big life questions revealed. That's because this mission is the very essence of you.

This is a very important step, so I want you to do this in a way that is impactful for you. I bet you already know what you believe your mission is. You may not have thought of crystalizing it in a statement. Some of the suggestions I'm about to give you will be helpful in defining what is important to you and how the way you parent is an extension of all you are. Your mission statement will be an overall goal incorporating your expectations, your mom style and your intentions to accomplish them.

Where do you begin?

Mommy

- Start with the big picture then you can narrow your focus to get crystal clear.

- I urge you to pick your deal breakers first. This may seem an odd place to start. You may be thinking of all the things you hope for as a parent and haven't given any thought to the negatives you may encounter or ones you want to avoid. This is part of the preparedness that is vital.

I'm a huge believer in the value of knowing what you don't want before you can know what you truly do want.

I call this *The Elimination Theory.*

Get the noes out of the way to find your yeses.

Then those will be guideposts you can look to time and time again. This will also keep you from being sidetracked by the distraction of things that aren't significant to your mission.

So where do you start to do that? Declaring your mission will mean thinking back again on the parts of your family legacy that didn't serve you well. There are things you know for certain you want to eliminate from your child's story.

- Is there a parenting method you definitely will not implement?

Mommy Missions, Mantras, & Mandates

This is an echo of the expectations evaluation to include here. Maybe this goes back to something you experienced. It could be something as destructive as physical or emotional abuse. In that case, the path is clear that you must discontinue such unacceptable behavior and break that pattern of violence. Period. This is non-negotiable.

Then there are parenting practices that can be much less intense but still impactful. For example, a standby response many moms use for cooperation is *because I told you so*. Or worse, *because you're the child and I'm the adult*. Now that may sound innocuous enough, but to a child it can mean the difference between depending on someone else to lead the way or learning to think independently.

It can have more far-reaching effects. Teaching a child that adults have blanket authority can mean making your child susceptible to being manipulated by an authority figure. They must learn to respect authority but be strong enough to defend themselves. See how something that sounds mundane can be more pervasive in its effect?

- Have you seen how other moms have made missteps that you want to avoid? I believe in the value of success modeling. Part of that again is elimination. Much can be learned from observing the techniques of others and accessing their effectiveness.

Mommy

Haven't you ever been at the mall and seen a mother scolding their worn-out child and thought how they should have been more patient or more conscious of the child's limitations for endless shopping?

How about that uncomfortable feeling when you are in restaurant and a mom is allowing their child to disrupt everyone in the dining room with food throwing and chair hopping?

Inappropriate behavior can often be sourced to a parent not being mindful of the child's limits for stress. It can also be the lack of clear rules and consistency. Certainly, there are battles of wills when a child tends to be more defiant. You can relate.

Later on, it might be about the parents who allow their teenage children to drink alcohol or let them off with a wink and a nod on the things that are a matter of integrity and honesty. It starts early.

Now is the perfect time to begin to establish your stand on these issues.

Once you've gotten the don'ts out of the way, let's talk about what you do want as a mom. What kind of childhood do you envision for your child? What do you want them to say years from now was their childhood experience?

Mommy Missions, Mantras, & Mandates

You can make your plan as broad or as detailed as you like. You may have dozens of ideas or rules or guidelines that you want to follow. I had a client who wrote pages and pages full of her thoughts. She made them into an affirmation journal to stay focused on her mission.

I am a lover of words but an admirer of saying more with less. To help my mom clients kick start their plan I often ask them to put it into twenty words or less like an elevator pitch. Get basic and build from there.

Here's a good one.

I will make every effort not to screw up.

Good place to start, right? That's about as worthy and earnest as you can get. Deep at your center you're praying for that above all. The rest is icing.

As you develop your plan try to get as close to the core values as you can from the beginning. That will give you a blueprint for the rest. Those core values are the framework of the life you are building for you child. The stronger you make it, the studier it will be to support them in the early years and sustain them as they mature. Legacy is the foundation, and you are pouring that footing for them. It's a big job but you are more than capable. It's also exciting

Mommy

to think *you* are providing the best possible chance your child has for happiness and success.

Here's my personal mommy mantra.

I will do all things and make all decisions for this child from a place of honor and love.

That has been my mandate since the day I looked into my firstborn's eyes. She gave me a look that said, *here I am, I trust you.*

I took that as literally as I could and made my promise that has never altered from that mission.

I have taken missteps, made mistakes, and miscalculated.

I've faced difficult situations and dealt with heartache. None of those has ever been long-lasting because my intent was rooted in that mission.

I've also watched with satisfaction and pride as my efforts have resulted in joyous successes. I've laughed and danced and had my heart soar. That core commitment remains my cornerstone.

I encourage you to get as much clarity as you can as early as possible

Mommy Missions, Mantras, & Mandates

to lay this solid groundwork. It will give you a head-start and serve you when you need direction.

If you have teenagers and think it's too late to do this, I want you to know this.

Today is the earliest you can begin anything.

Don't think about time lost. Think about time left.

Do this today.

When you face the inevitable moments when you don't know what to do you will have this declaration as a reminder of your intent, a direction for moving forward to get you where you know you want to go.

Please consider this. People talk in terms of ages and stages and phases kids go through as if each one was descriptive of a completely different creature. It's as if babies were one type. Then young children are another and teenagers might as well be a separate species altogether.

Remember they're human beings with all the rights and privileges as such from the very moment they come into your life. Consider that as you go. They're tiny people but their needs and wants are

Mommy

no smaller than anyone else's no matter their age. Their beautiful amazing little brains and hearts think and feel and experience joy and hurt the same as all humans.

They may know less than you, but they don't *feel* less.

CHAPTER 9

Call in the Reinforcements

As a mom you will need help.

There's no shame in that.

*You **are** capable.*

*You **are** worthy of this assignment you've been given.*

What you need to form is not just a support system but a circle of support. That denotes not only a resource but a form of protection. Think of a moat that encircles and protects or the term "circling the wagons" as an expression of defense against outside or hostile forces. A circle is continuous and reciprocal. You will give as much as you give and in that you receive again and again. Everyone benefits.

My wish for you is that your mother is there for you in every way to guide you. That's the natural order of things and how it *should* work generationally.

If you're really fortunate, your mother-in-law is supportive.

If you have these foremothers in your life, please receive what they bring to the table in wisdom and love even when it is difficult to hear.

This is where we need to talk about the mother-daughter dynamic. Now that you're a mom you will begin to look at your mother in a new light. A realization that she's been where you are in this moment will make you see the things that she did for you that you may not have appreciated before. It may also bring a recognition that she did things that you now believe are not the way you want to parent.

That's the beauty of your turn to be the mother. You get to decide *everything* about how you will parent. Remember your child is counting on you to use your life experiences to ensure their safety and happiness. Challenge yourself to really give some thought to this. It may also offer an opportunity for healing if there is a space between you and your mom keeping you from sharing this experience.

This is an exceptional chance to experience your mom in a way that will enhance both of your lives immeasurably. For you moms

Call in the Reinforcements

who are parenting your grown children as they become parents themselves, I implore you to make your best efforts to be their champion. It is a fabulous opportunity to continue your mission statement for the next generation.

Having your mom as a mentor is special, but you want to have the camaraderie of moms your age as you go along. They are the definitive tribe. They're your best source for knowledge and reassurance that what is happening in your mom world is universal. You need someone to laugh with you and not dismiss your concerns.

Someone who doesn't question your tears or your fears.

There are days you feel alone. You may be physically alone and feel lonely, but remember you're a member of a huge club. There are millions of moms globally and chances are many are just like you feeling exactly in this moment what you're feeling. You need to seek out and find your tribe. The support of people who are like-minded and share your belief systems is invaluable. For your sanity that support is essential.

Social media has provided many outlets for mommy groups. If you find one or more that nourish you and lift you up, then by all means use that outlet. If you're a newbie mom, I caution you that some groups can be a tough audience. If you've been on social media in mommy groups, you know all about this.

Mommy

Mommy shaming is never acceptable.

Never do it or allow yourself to be a target.

There is no scorecard for parenting except your satisfaction and the happiness of your child. Period.

The other problem is misinformation. You're so eager to do the right thing that in searching for answers, you will encounter as much misguided or misleading information as useable advice. This is where your common sense and intuition come in. Mothers have a built-in radar. Some are closely attuned to it and can access it easily. Others have to work a bit more to get in touch with it and tap in. That's okay. There are ways to do that. Read, watch, listen. There are some good books and articles. There is great modeling going on around you if you look. You can hear the sounds of happy moms and their children or those who are miserable. Watch for what's working for others.

Finding other moms that you identify with and want to be around is a lot like when you were searching for your mate. It's all chemistry. Mom-buddies are special. They know when to hold each other accountable and when to cut each other slack. They're happy for you when you triumph and have your back when you stumble. Most importantly, they are there to lift you when you fall.

When you find one of these lovely creatures, hold them close and

Call in the Reinforcements

offer them your love and care in reciprocal. Not everyone will be all of that for you. It only takes one to get you through.

You have mommy friends that are in your life because they're your neighbors or part of playgroups, dance lessons, sports, church, and school. These are association relationships. You encounter these moms as part of your child's experiences. These are much like extended familial relationships. You marry into another family and gain relatives when your siblings marry or choose partners.

Blended families produced by divorce and remarriages bring new relationships to navigate. They come with the territory. You choose the territory not always the participants. Often times you get lucky and find a great mom-buddy within these groups. Wonderful bonds can be made and grown on the common ground of your child's interests.

These are also opportunities for comparison and competition. Moms can be fiercely competitive about their kids.

Remember that protective is not competitive.

You should always protect your child, but there is room for everyone's child to shine without casting a shadow on yours or the reverse.

We've talked about the people around you, but let's look closer. If you have a partner or spouse you've got a great source of support. The key is to ask for their help and input. It is critical that you be clear about your expectations about when and what you need. You deserve that. If you don't have their commitment, then insist on it. Every job has resources for helping performance. Being a mother should be no different.

Consider your resources. Ask yourself some discovery questions about that.

- Do you recognize that you need support for this very important job?

- Do you let your desire to be strong and capable prevent you from leaning in to support from others?

- Do you have a supportive relationship with your mother?

- Will you consider opening that relationship more if need be?

- Will you ask her for her input and assistance?

- If you don't have a relationship with your mom, is there some other person that you can call on as a supporter and mentor?

- Can you open your heart to your mother-in-law if she's willing?

Call in the Reinforcements

- Don't forget about your siblings as resources as well. Aunts and uncles are wonderful sources of support for you and your child. If your siblings are parents, there is much they offer from their experiences as well.

- Are you tapping into the other moms around you as a support system?

- Do you have a real mom-buddy whose support is undeniable and steadfast?

- Are you willing to be that for someone else?

- Are you encouraging the other moms around you to look to you for their support? Often times you miss a meaningful connection simply because of a lack of outreach. It is a reciprocal relationship. Someone needs your support as much as you need theirs.

- Do you have siblings to bring into your support circle?

- Have you established your expectations from your partner with them clearly?

- Are you clear with yourself what your needs are and how you expect others to help?

Mommy

- Can you be honest with yourself on this issue without blame or shame or self-condemnation?

I'm so excited to be along for your ride. Count me in as part of your reinforcement team!

In the next sections, I'll address specific ages and stages that you may be in right now. One ties into the next because everything you do matters. Behavior is built on experiences. Once you understand the role you play in your child's behavior patterns you can begin to see your way to the future you want. Parenting a grade schooler is different than tiny ones. Tweeners have their own issues. Teenagers seem like aliens. You think by the time you get them to college you're on the downhill side of your mom job.

Surprise!

Now you relate to them as the person you've helped them to become.

With young adult children you begin a whole new phase of their life and yours. Everything you continue to do continues to matter to you both. Your relationship is dependent upon your willingness to continue to do your job full out.

Your mission never ends.

Call in the Reinforcements

Now let's talk about that fabulous kiddo or kiddos of yours and get some practical strategies for getting this job done!

PART TWO:

BABIES, TODDLERS, & PRESCHOOLERS, OH MY!

CHAPTER 10

Little Ones

Now you want some specifics about the mechanics of this job.

Basics to build on. That's the point. They matter now because they affect what happens later.

I want you to do this mommy job your way. But I know like any on the job training you've got questions and concerns. and you're looking for tips on successful practices for the everyday routine parts of your mom job. I have plenty that I believe in because they have worked for me and others I have counseled. Some I learned by trial and error. Many I chose because I have studied childhood development and I am passionate about emotional wellness that I believe begins in childhood.

SMALL CHILDREN ARE SIMPLY SMALL HUMANS.

They have all the needs and rights and expectations for happiness that all people have no matter their age. Quite frankly, the younger

Mommy

they are the easier it is to satisfy those needs with consistency and care. It's your physical energy and patience that will be taxed the most. Later as they grow up and become more aware of the world outside your home their wants will increase accordingly. But when they're little, you are their only information source.

Because I refrain from using qualifiers for these choices other than to say I do believe they are successful practices, I find it helpful to talk in terms of what works. Good or bad, right or wrong ways of doing things are for you to decide for you, your child, your family, and your life as long as they do not endanger your child physically or emotionally.

I respect that everyone comes at any situation in their life from different viewpoints based on those factors we discussed earlier. Family legacy, personal wiring, life location, relationships and experiences you bring to the mommy table influence your mommy style.

You hear about picking your battles. Wow, that sounds ominous. Who wants to go to war?

Try to think of it as picking your issues. Some things matter to you that aren't of concern for someone else. This is the *"you"* part of this job.

What matters to you.

Little Ones

I want to help you keep the issues from becoming battles. Sometimes a subtle shift is all that's needed. A little hack can make all the difference. The main thing is to contain the disruption to your life. Putting your foot down now and doing the work to get through a phase as easily a possible can keep you from a long-term consequence. Do you put in a short intense effort for a difficult phase to pass or do you let it continue and possibly escalate and have it as an issue in your life long-term? Think of ripping off the Band-Aid. Quick pain fades faster.

Please remember I am not mommy-shaming you in any way if you have a different style as long as it keeps your child's interest at heart. If there's one thing I know about moms is their unlimited capacity to be creative with their love.

Whether you are a freshly minted mommy or a long hauler with years of experience, it is worth revisiting your first days on the job. I bet you can remember it like it was yesterday.

Your first few days are literally consumed with the how-to practices for the food and shelter part of caring for a baby. The diapers, baby wipes, diaper rash preventative ointment applications, burping, feedings, all become ritualistic second nature performance. One minute you can't believe anyone with a medical degree would entrust this newborn into your rookie hands. They went to school for a dozen years to learn this stuff. You've read a couple of books. The next minute that baby is snoozing away, and you feel totally

Mommy

confident. You've got this. The next thing you know you're up at two am changing the wet sheets and their onesie for the fifth time you start to wonder again if you can do this.

Then one day as you're going about those tasks, you look into your baby's eyes and they smile. Right at you! In that moment what you intellectually knew was true about being responsible for their comfort and necessities resonates in your brain and the realization that their happiness is yours to deliver hits you in the heart.

Let's talk about some guidelines and suggestions that will help. Some may have come to you intuitively already and some may seem logical once you consider them. Some you might not have thought about before in any way other than instructional. There's a reason behind the way they work.

These are based on basic early childhood developmental markers. But their impact can be far reaching and can shape how this mommy job goes for you in terms of your happiness and satisfaction with the results and in terms of emotional wellness for your child.

These may seem like practical rules, but know that everything I address has a psychological component that concerns your child's emotional development. That's a huge point that I want to get across to you.

Little Ones

Everything you do matters.

Everything.

Like dominos, each practice leans against the others for support. Each practice has an effect on the next. Cumulatively they shape your child. Now that is an awesome burden. It's also an exciting mandate.

You signed up for this job so let's get to the basics of building this strong foundation.

The Beginning

This first one is so basic but so important. The practice will benefit you forever.

From day one, make eye contact as often as you possibly can. This seems simple, but the importance of bonding can't be over-emphasized. Begin establishing direct eye contact as a standard practice in your communication. It's a factor right now in their development and sets the foundation for growth in their communication style.

Start now and it becomes routine.

Why does that matter?

Mommy

It establishes respect.

It cements trust.

It teaches courtesy.

It encourages empathy. You can't feel what you don't see.

Once your baby becomes a toddler, they will be much more likely to listen to direction when they routinely make eye contact while you're talking. In fact, always insist they look at you when you are giving instructions or direction, especially when correcting behavior. It establishes your authority and mutual respect for the communication process.

When you look your child in the eye, they know they have your attention as well.

This is an invaluable connection to establish that will benefit your relationship and communication along the entire timeline as they grow older. Start the practice between you now. It will become a habit that will serve you well.

Think if you only had one channel on your TV or only one show you could stream on your devices.

That's what you are to your infant.

Little Ones

You're the feed on their bandwidth.

- You are your baby's major source of stimuli. That means their brain is depending on you to activate it and get those synapsis firing. Talk to them constantly. The sound of your voice has been with them since before they were born. It's like a lullaby to them. Think on that a moment. Wow, right? Speak to them with that in mind.

- You have your baby's undivided attention. You're like their own personal one-woman show. You wow them with everything you do!

- Your face is the most important sight to your baby. They watch it for clues and cues. Use your eyes and smile to connect. They learn communication skills directly from you.

- Remember your baby thinks you are the most beautiful person in the world. Isn't that a lovely thought?

- Establish a routine and stick to it when you can. Teething, colic, colds, the dog barking, the doorbell, the yardmen mowing outside beneath the nursery window will all interrupt that often, but when you can, make your life easier with a schedule.

- Speaking of dogs, I have to include this very important tip. I know you love your dog. I understand that because I adore

Mommy

mine. I get that they are family members. In fact, you may have referred to your dog as your baby before you got a human one.

Your dog may have accepted your new baby into their space perfectly as far as you can see. They may even seem protective. They love each other and you want them to be best buddies.

I know your dog and your baby are adorable together and they are a YouTube viral hit with millions of views waiting to happen, but a dog, as fabulous and smart as they are, is still an animal with instincts we don't always know or understand.

Please don't let your dog close to your baby's face.

One of my daughters was bitten millimeters below her eye when she was only a year old by a sweet family dog with no prior history of aggression. She had been around this dog almost daily.

I know you think your dog would never do that.

I don't want you to be proven wrong by a scar on your baby's gorgeous face.

Remember also you certainly can't predict the behavior of someone else's dog. If your child is accustomed to getting close

Little Ones

to their dog's face for puppy love they might choose the wrong dog to kiss.

Even in the mundane rituals and basics of child-care there are always emotional components to consider. Break it down.

Your young child is one big walking heart.

They feel everything.

Everything matters to them.

You affect their everything.

I always say if children came into the world as toddlers, I would have had ten of them. I can tell you why.

No one loves as purely, as totally, as open heartedly, as freely as an eighteen-month-old.

They laugh at your silly faces, are wowed by your Play Doh artistry, don't care if you shower or brush your hair, never mention the extra pounds you carry or the cellulite that has suddenly appeared on the backs of your thighs, think you are the smartest person on the planet, and don't complain when the dishes pile up or the dust bunnies multiply in the corners of the room.

Mommy

They forgive instantly and forget your mistakes even faster.

In many ways, they are the person you wish you were.

And they have the grace to love you as if you are.

They look at you as if you're the center of the universe.

You are.

The center of *their* universe.

You think they have your heart wrapped around their little fingers.

Then you realize you hold their tiny little hearts in your hands.

Let's talk about something no one likes to discuss.

Sometimes despite all your efforts and even your pleas your infant's fussiness will escalate and seem inconsolable. You try everything but nothing works.

Babies cry.

A lot.

Little Ones

They have a way of doing it so often and for so long in such a way that it can feel like some sort of mind game torture.

You're exhausted.

You've got one raw nerve left.

And you feel it unraveling with every wail.

This frustration you're feeling does not diminish your love for your child. It does not mean you aren't a fabulous mother. It does not mean you are failing at this job.

It means your baby is doing what babies do.

Your crying baby isn't trying to get under your skin.

They have no malicious intent.

No agenda to machinate.

They cry because they're uncomfortable for a myriad of reasons that you may or may not be able to identify. They even begin to develop emotional responses and sometimes they simply get mad for some reason just like you do. But they can't articulate their feelings except in one primal way.

Mommy

They cry.

And cry.

And cry.

Now, to help you in these incredibly stressful moments, I'm giving you a coping strategy that can be used from infancy to forever in all manner of emotional moments with a child when their dissatisfaction gets out of control and you feel as though you are losing it.

I want you to wait.

W.A.I.T.

This is a simple acronym.

Walk. Take a few steps back. Move yourself away.

Allow. Let your mind to catch up to the emotion of the moment.

Inhale. Take a deep breath to clear your head.

Take. Take sixty seconds. One short minute of time to talk to yourself can dial down the drama.

When you give yourself physical space by stepping back you have

Little Ones

interrupted the reflex to have any semblance of inappropriate physical contact with your child.

We all know the feeling that can overtake any rational person when pushed to their limit.

Anger born of frustration is a mighty challenger for rationality.

You may have an impulse to shake a baby when rocking or walking doesn't do the trick in trying to calm them. It only takes seconds to damage a baby brain.

Later on, you may have an urge to spank your stubborn two-year-old or smack your defiant grade schooler or slap your sassy-mouthed teenager.

Your feelings are justified.

Acting on them physically is not.

The speed of emotion is faster than the speed of reasoning.

I'm going to repeat that a lot.

A great deal of the time your mom job is a series of frustrations. Some big and some small. Give yourself time and space for a few seconds to let reason prevail.

Mommy

Throughout your mom job you will be ineffective trying to teach your child anything with any method other than by example. If you hit your child, they will learn that hitting back is an appropriate answer to anger. I have to hold back from approaching a parent when I see them spanking a child for hitting a playmate or their sibling.

The irony isn't lost on your child.

They will bully when bullied.

CHAPTER 11

Sleeping

Sleep has become the newest wellness topic. There are special mattresses, pillows, sheets, weighted blankets, aromatherapy, and melatonin supplements. There are theories about when and what to eat for proper sleep, what hours are best, what to put in your bath water to induce sleep, and the importance of putting away the screen devices in your life at bedtime.

There're podcasts to tell you bedtime stories, apps to calm your nerves, audio books to download, TikTok sleep influencers, and soothing teas to drink. There are experts who have become millionaires telling you how to do one of the most natural, instinctive, necessary human functions. Sleep has become an industry.

Mommies are OBSESSED with sleep.

You can't help it.

It's all you think about during these years. In fact, you think about it even when you're sleeping, which probably isn't very often. It is singularly the most important thing in your life because you need it and so does your child. Your life is centered around when you can get them to sleep and for how long and when you can get some. It becomes the marker for everything else because you have to schedule your life around it to some degree or another if you want to develop any kind of schedule or routine you can count on.

I've known high-power moms who make elaborate spreadsheets detailing sleep activities. I've seen countless blogs, posts, articles, and books. I've heard of suggestions like aromatherapy, black-out shades, white noise machines, night lights, no night lights, swaddling, sleep sacks, rocking, no rocking, pacifiers, no pacifiers, and baby message techniques.

I've known of moms who take the opposite approach and have no sleep plan or schedule at all. They are perfectly fine with not having any sort of method to the chaos that unpredictability causes. God love you if that's you, but there's no way I could do that. I have to have some control over my life's course and some structure.

From a developmental standpoint, I believe structured sleep is beneficial to your child. They need sleep for proper growth. They need structure for developing good habits.

I highly recommend schedules rigid enough to have some semblance of predictable lifestyle but flexible enough to keep you from losing your mind with adherence.

Sleeping

You need structure for your sanity. Sleep issues are one of the most prominent early childhood concerns.

So, here's where I give you some mom-to-mom advice based on my experiences and my observation of the experiences of others that will help you in these earliest years and set you up for sleep success later on.

- You've heard it before but someone telling you not to let the baby sleep in bed with you sounds reasonable until your little one keeps you up all night with their crying. I know the feeling of exasperation that leaves you vulnerable to the path of least resistance. You put that warm little infant body next to you and almost immediately they quiet and settle down. You're comfy stretched out on your own sheets on your nice pillow and all is right with the world as you both get some peace and quiet. I hear you saying, *who cares as long as I get some sleep in this moment?* I know it's hard but with an infant this is extremely dangerous. Trust me, sitting with a young dad who tragically rolled over on his baby son while asleep and helping that dad over the guilt is excruciating. It happens.

- Toddlers are adorable. Especially sleepy ones in the middle of the night. I mean they have that funny bedhead hair and those drowsy eyes that plead for you to say *yes, come on and get in.* But a toddler in your bed at night can cause all sorts of problems. All that cuteness is a cover-up for their stubborn, resistant defiance that's matched only by your frustration. You must resist their crafty ways.

This habit can start from infancy or long after your child is old enough that the danger of a roll-over accident has passed. The danger at this stage lies in the disruption to your adult sleep (and other grown-up activities!) quality and your child's dependency issues.

This can also be the beginning of forfeiting your authority. That may not seem like a big deal when it's a toddler but what about the teenager your child will be one day? As dramatic as that may sound in this moment think about the fact that you're setting the scene for your future by giving in now.

Allowing your child to sleep in your room or in your bed on special occasions is a different story. It can be fun to have a "slumber party" now and then. This is very different than a habit or act of noncompliance with your rules.

- There are lots of tricks to get your toddler to sleep in their own bed. Decorative night lights, choosing a special favorite animal as a sleep buddy, buying character themed bedding, a favorite pillow, glow-in-the-dark stars on the ceiling. You know those already.

    Let's take it a little further. Let them have a vote in what you use

Sleeping

as an incentive. Don't you like to have a vote in the things that affect you? Give that option to your child. Let them choose.

That can extend to allowing them to have a voice in other things in their environment. I believe making your child's space in your home whether it's their own bedroom, or their part of a shared room, feel like an extension of them is so important. It's the beginning of autonomy. Giving them a say even if it's as simple as which shelf the books go on or where each stuffed animal goes on the bed is a boon to self-confidence.

They live in world where most of the things that surround them belong to others. Ownership begets responsibility. It's never too early to establish their sense of self in tangible ways. It's also the beginning of analytical thinking and the first step to decision making. Besides, everyone wants to believe their opinion counts. Making simple decisions and having them validated by you has far-reaching benefits.

- Institute scheduled bedtime rituals. You've heard this one, but have you thought about why it's important? Life is about structured existence. Civilization exits within set parameters. There are procedures to everything you do in everyday life, in school, your job, your relationships, your community. Learning that there are patterns to follow for successful functioning is imperative. Accepting that compliance can be a component for success is key to a child grasping that concept.

Mommy

Something like choosing pajamas, brushing teeth, selecting and reading a short book or two (limit the number and stick to it), turning on the music and the night light, prayers, hugs and a kiss in the same order every night to establish an expected routine. Kids LOVE routine. It's security for them. They begin to gain confidence in the tiniest accomplishments. Following a schedule with expected rituals feels like mission accomplished especially if you praise them on their success.

- Another way to begin to encourage self-reliance is by allowing your toddler to choose their clothes for the next day from two outfits you decide are appropriate. (Did you think I had forgotten that they can't match tops and bottoms at this age?) That way they have controlled choices but ones they feel they make independently.

Choosing clothing is a great opportunity to talk about the weather outside and the seasons and the miracles of nature. It's an opportunity to teach colors and patterns and textures without feeling at all like instruction. It's one of those simple tasks that can provide learning opportunities.

It really takes so little to spark a young child's interest. You'll never know the full impact of your input to your child's imagination through the mundane motions of everyday life.

CHAPTER 12

Feeding

Food is a basic human need. You have to eat. It's also one of the most emotionally charged requirements. We place value on it. All sorts of feelings center on food and meals. Think of how certain smells activate your memory. The sight or even the thought of others conjure recall of places or people or situations.

Food is much more than nourishment.

From the first day they're in the world, you're constantly thinking about when your child's going to eat, what you're going to feed them, and how much they consume. You measure success in ounces of food intake.

You'll continue to monitor their nourishment for as long as they live with you. That's years you'll think about feeding your child.

You may not have thought about how much you influence how they feel about food because it's such a constant in your day-to-day

Mommy

interaction. Here again is a place that from the beginning makes a difference.

It's easy to use food as a reward with kids.

It's easy to fall into a pattern where they learn to use it to manipulate you.

How big an issue food becomes in your relationship is dependent on you. Let's talk about feeding.

- You've already made a decision about breastfeeding vs bottle. Organic options and homemade food vs store bought. All of that is your choice for nutrition. When it comes to eating and mealtime, structure and order are important to establishing healthy food associations.

- Mealtime should be set up as a pleasurable time not a battlefield. Food can be a pawn in the mommy-child game. You get to decide to what degree you will play.

  Don't get hung up on the food pyramid. Being freaked out about food is a waste of time and energy. Kids' eating preferences change very quickly. If they are growing properly and making their developmental markers, then cut yourself and them some slack.

Feeding

It's my personal opinion that conflicts over food are more destructive than any nutritional benefits your child may miss the few months or even years that they want to limit their palate.

- Encourage your child to respect the act of sharing a meal. Make it about mealtime not the food. Use it as time to talk and engage them in it as a family activity even if it has to be on the run. A set time around the table is wonderful but not necessary for nourishment or development. It isn't always possible to have a traditional meal, but it is a nice goal. Like lots of things with young children, adaptation is key to harmony.

- As for snacking, you know what's healthy. You know Skittles are not the best choice when whole wheat Cheerios will do. You also know the humiliation of showing up at the park with a bag of Doritos when your friend gives her toddler a container of carrot sticks. Isn't it strange the way foods can make you feel about yourself? Your child will not develop a dreaded disease if they eat the Doritos so lighten up. Choose healthy when you can but let it go if your toddler refuses hummus. It is not a reflection on you. It's on the chickpeas.

There isn't much a kid won't do for a cookie. (Me, too!) Conversely, food issues and denial to cooperate with your eating demands can set up a dynamic for food and eating compliance or noncompliance as manipulation. That can lead to big consequences later on.

Mommy

Food and eating should be about nourishment not emotion at this age. This can apply to both undereating and overeating.

Balance is key.

Food is good fuel not a friend or an enemy.

Learning an appreciation for food and even food preparation is healthy. And moms, please be vigilant and watch what you say about your own body image and your relationship with food. It's so easy to talk out loud about your weight or how you look. Without realizing it you may be assigning a negative connotation to foods by admonishing yourself for eating them. Those are probably foods your child views as delicious and desirable like breads and sweets. Don't set up food struggles with conflicting messages.

There's a way to talk about moderating intake, yours and theirs, that's about what's good for you nutritionally not what's bad for your weight or body shape.

Your child is watching and listening and mirroring your nutritional behavior and your valuations. Even your toddler.

CHAPTER 13

Developmental Skills

You've scoured all of the baby books and memorized the growth charts. You've read dozens of mommy blogs. You're constantly watching for all the signs of "normal" development in your child. Anxiety consumes you when their supposed milestone month comes and goes without them accomplishing whatever development step is next on the list.

Your child is a person not a statistic.

They will develop at their own pace.

This is not a race between your best friend's child, your sister's child, your neighbor's child, the kid on your favorite TV show or a TikTok tot with a million views and your child. There are skills that develop along a pattern for most kids but if your child lags a bit it's no cause for panic. Conversely, if your child begins to talk

Mommy

much earlier than most that's no cause to assume that they are a candidate for a MIT scholarship.

However, you can often affect their timing with your encouragement and attention.

- Talk intentionally to your child. This again sounds like a simple and logical practice but often times it's easy to forget. Every word you offer your child is a gesture of your time and attention.

- You can spark your child's imagination by fueling their curiosity. Encourage questions. Ask questions. Engage. Engage. Engage.

- As a mom you spend countless hours in the car shuttling your child to all manner of appointments, lessons, and school later on. It's easy to turn up the music or play a cartoon or movie on the car's entertainment system to keep them occupied. Think of it as an opportunity to have their undivided attention. Use it. They are a captive audience. Engage them in conversation. Talk with them.

  Using car time can be intentional and educational without feeling forced. Point out the changing leaves or the squirrels gathering acorns or the daffodils lining fences or the shapes of the clouds as ways to teach are subtle and effective.

- I know the phone is a mighty strong temptation for those hours

Developmental Skills

in the car. I LOVE MY PHONE. I run my business and personal life from my cell phone. I remind myself every day to put it down and keep it down in the car. With teenage drivers in my life again, I have made the rule of no texting while driving a policy I practice in an effort to influence them and my littlest one who will have heard it a million times before she gets her license!

I get it. I have logged hundreds of thousands of miles in my car hauling kids from here to there. I can't even fathom the hours, all done in a flurry of getting someplace on time and with all the necessary sports equipment, science fair projects, birthday gifts, sleeping bags, school lunches, backpacks, bikes, scooters, skateboards, helmets and rain gear in tow.

Take the time to make all the car time beneficial. Turn the grind into gold.

CHAPTER 14

Fun & Games

There is no easier audience to entertain than a toddler. Despite all of the commercials and ads you see toddlers do not require flashing lights and sound effects. Any seasoned mom knows all of the stuff you buy them will be forgotten by the time they reach preschool if not before.

Resist buying all the latest greatest stuff.

Save your money.

The older your child gets, the more expensive their wish list. Big kids equal big-ticket items. Let's talk about the benefits of fun and games.

- Curiosity is like a muscle. The more you use it the stronger it becomes. You worry about your child getting enough physical exercise so be concerned that their curiosity gets exercised as well.

Mommy

- Curiosity is the beginning of all discovery. Use what's around you and they'll translate that into learning to be resourceful. Being resourceful is a cornerstone of creativity.

- Don't forget puzzles. They not only stimulate the brain they promote hand-eye coordination, fine motor skills, shape recognition, concentration and focus, spatial awareness, goal setting, persistence, memory, confidence, and patience.

   Life is a puzzle. You have to figure things out. Problem solving and the self-confidence that comes from completing a task can begin with learning from puzzles.

- Choose age-appropriate games and puzzles. Nothing can squash a child's self-esteem as quickly as a failed attempt to complete or participate in what should be fun.

- A small child can begin to learn impulse control when you give them limits on what they can and can't have in the moment.

- Especially with toddlers and little kids the ease with which they can be entertained and satisfied is remarkable. They're an easy sell on making something that isn't a game feel like fun. Unloading the lower rack of the dishwasher, bathing the dog, washing the car, separating socks by color, counting the elbows in the mac and cheese box. This can be the beginning of

Fun & Games

learning that life's rewards and pleasures aren't always available to order online.

- You'll have times when you think if you have to make one more playdough snake, have one more Barbie wedding, build one more Lego tower, pour one more imaginary cup of tea, watch one more Sesame Street episode, sing one more Disney song you'll scream. Take a breath and remind yourself this is a moment you will wish for before you know it.

Since we're talking entertainment, let's have the screen time talk.

If you have a newborn, you're thinking, *Becki what are you talking about? That's years away for me.*

Trust me, you *will* be tempted to use your devices for instant entertainment and convenience before you know it.

I get it. If you could just keep that toddler of yours occupied for a few minutes you could finish that call or dinner or the laundry or catch a break for a second.

That shiny flashing mini machine is perfect for that. And toddlers love them.

Then there are the times you're out to dinner and the meal is taking too long to arrive or you'd like desert and coffee, but your

Mommy

toddler is restless. The magical musical rectangle is the quick and easy answer.

You'll have to think about that and make decisions for your child about screens. You've heard the cautions and you have to form your own opinion about where you stand on this issue. Allow me a few lines here to state my case.

Those marvelous little brains are so precious.

I grew up in the earlier years of television. Some people thought it would ruin the minds and eyes of my generation. It didn't. But it did serve as a babysitter much more than I think was desirable or beneficial. We grew dependent on it to inform us, entertain us, and keep us company. Did watching hours of cartoons and afternoon programs damage me? Probably not, but I wasn't playing outside or spending time with my mom either.

My concern about modern screen time is the overstimulation and the neurobiology yet to be determined. But more than that, I know how much babies and toddlers learn from facial cues, especially from their mothers.

My hope is that you would opt for that sort of one-on-one stimulation over the illumination of blue light.

Give them the glow of your beautiful expression-filled face instead.

Fun & Games

But remember in order to do that you will have to put your phone down. If your child sees that screen in your hand constantly, they will mimic that behavior later on.

Short term action for long term benefit.

Your toddler will become a preschooler then a grade schooler then a pre-teen then a teen and you will find yourself complaining about all their screen time. It will be easier to state your case and ween them off if you don't get them started on the habit so early. And if you have modeled restraint by restricting your use in front of them.

Okay, I had my say. Thank you for listening.

Here's something else I have to say about entertaining your little one. One of the most vital forms of entertainment you can offer a child is a book. Please hear me on this one.

This is way more than about keeping them occupied for a few moments.

If you want your child to do well in school and excel in life do one thing. Do it over and over and over.

READ. READ. READ.

Mommy

Then, READ to them some more!!!!!

This may be the simplest most powerful hack of all.

*Books hold the key to **everything**.*

Within books there is knowledge and wisdom, and insight, and understanding, and empathy, and adventure, and travel, and ideologies, and philosophies, and invention, and resources and discovery.

And companionship.

One of the greatest gifts you can give your child is the reverence and desire for books and the ability and privilege to read. It is a lasting gift.

If they value books, they will be more prepared for school. School curriculums are book-based. At every level all required knowledge and work performance is contingent on reading and comprehension skills. They'll have reading assignments for homework and summer reading lists to complete. You will be monitoring reading time for years.

You can eliminate a miserable future problem in school by taking a lack of reading skills out of the equation.

Fun & Games

Do yourself and your child a HUGE favor and treat books as treasures. If you present a book to a very young child as a fun treat, they will automatically assume the same attitude. Make one-on-one reading time seem like a special event every time and you will quickly see their enthusiasm grow.

Open a book and you open their eyes and their mind.

The world belongs to your child.

Nothing should be withheld from them.

Knowledge is their birthright.

They should never be denied all that is theirs.

Show them that they possess unlimited power in their imagination.

Tell them books are the portal to their potential.

You hold this key to their now and to their future.

Unlock the door to all their possibilities.

CHAPTER 15

Temper Tantrums & Melt Downs

Fact. Every little one has a temper tantrum. Or dozens of them.

You may think yours won't. Don't set yourself up for that big disappointment.

There's nothing quite as volatile as a temper tantrum. The room for escalation is huge for both you and your child. Here's where your child is depending on you to be the grown-up.

It's hard because you know the feelings your toddler is having so well. You often feel like throwing yourself onto the floor and beating it with your fists or stomping your feet in a huff of non-compliance. If you could get away with such behavior wouldn't it make you feel better? That's where you child is in the middle of a tantrum.

Mommy

As extreme as it may look, it feels so good in the moment to express the anger. Your child is looking for a release from the emotion that has rushed them and caused them discomfort.

You will often hear me say the speed of emotion is lightening quick.

Let me repeat it again.

The speed of emotion is faster than the speed of reason.

Every child has a meltdown and probably several over many stages. That's true for an adult and you have the ability to reason. A toddler or small child is only beginning to have a flicker of reasoning ability where their emotions are concerned. The difference with you and them is you have the knowledge of how to control it.

This isn't a matter of only your anger and theirs in the moment. It is a learning opportunity and the beginning of anger management for them.

To a toddler, the anger is bigger than them. They have nowhere to put it, so they let it out all over you. Why? Because you're the one they trust to have the answers and that you will help them with these feelings that overpower them.

- Respond with gentle understanding partnered with structured

Temper Tantrums & Melt Downs

recourse. Your toddler is depending on you to rescue them from themselves. They are out of control. They are relying on YOU to be the one in control. Why can't they just stop acting this way? They have no idea how to begin to get self-control until you offer clear guidelines and consequences. They react on pure impulse without reason.

The older they get the more the ability to reason will develop. The fastest way to insure that is to give them reasons why the behavior is unacceptable so they can begin to relate the behavior to the outcome.

- The most important first step to getting a temper tantrum under control is your reaction. That's the hard part, right? You can begin to deescalate this situation with a calm warning for your child to stop. Now I know this sounds like an impossible task and maybe even hollow advice given the anger and frustration that rise up and coarse through your body when this happens.

I speak from firsthand experience because all moms have had this experience. It can be tough. In a tantrum you know calmly telling them to stop will do nothing at first. You will have to tell them that the behavior is unacceptable, and it must stop several times before they hear you or act like they hear you.

Begging, though tempting, is not a good

Mommy

posture to ever hold with a child of any age.

You are the authority. Show it with strength in your voice and a clear plan of action. Trust me, if they know that you will react with calm resolve to stand your ground every time that they throw a tantrum, they'll soon realize the tantrum isn't the best way to get what they want.

- If your child is aggressive and hits others you punish them for that behavior, right? Then please think about that if you currently spank or use any form of hands-on discipline. I mentioned this when we talked about your frustration with infant crying. I must take a moment here to tell you that I personally find spanking to be in direct conflict with my mom philosophy. There are other ways to discipline. No matter the age I, find loss of possessions or privileges to be the most effective.

But what can you take from a toddler that will have impact? Think tangibles that matter to them. Removing favorite toys is a good one. Privileges at this age are things like getting to go to the park, visiting friends, tea party time, or backyard fun. I know you're saying *Becki then that means I'm limiting my freedom*. Again, I remind you that quick pain is worth the long-term alternative. You might have to stay home and miss out on a few things but in the long run it will be rewarded.

Temper Tantrums & Melt Downs

As they get older your child's priorities will be more and more evident and useful for this purpose. Once the unacceptable behavior stops you return whatever you removed. Then the idea of actions and consequences begins to be a concrete concept in their mind. I suggest that as part of this follow through after the tantrum is over is to take a moment to recap the event and go over the scene again. In just a few sentences while they are clear and calm you can reiterate your reasoning and reinforce your expectations.

- A temper tantrum in public is humiliating. No doubt. That can fuel your anger in your response. The question of what to do when your toddler throws a tantrum in front of others is answered best with another question. What's the first thing you should do? Your child's feelings must be addressed first to deescalate the situation.

  But what about the people witnessing the tantrum? Take a moment to think about it. Anyone watching knows this scenario well because every parent has experienced one up close and personally. Those folks are more merciful that you think.

  If anyone shames you with their stares, shake it off. These witnesses don't know you. They aren't significant in your life. Walk away and leave their judgement behind.

Mommy

Providing your child with the guidance they need for healthy development is far more important than what others think.

- After the drama dies down, take a moment to acknowledge your child's feelings. Remind them that you get angry, too. Tell them you've felt the same way and validate them as you reinforce the need for them to recognize their part in the situation. Make sure that they know their behavior was unacceptable, but they are loved.

- Sometimes a child simply has a meltdown. You know the feeling. It's when everything gets to be too much. Instead of exploding, it's as if the emotions grind to a halt and everything inside says *I give up. I've had it. This is bigger than me so I'm shutting down.* Then the emotions back up because you aren't releasing them. Think of it as a dam and the dam finally breaks from the pressure of the build up. The tears flow and with them comes all the emotion. In fact, I refer to it as an emotion dump. You can't hold it in, so it has to come flooding out. Kids have them. Moms have them. The best antidote is permission to let it out and a reassuring hug.

CHAPTER 16

Acting Out

Does the sun rise every day in the east?

Yep.

Can you count on it to happen?

Yep.

Will your child act out from time to time?

Yep.

Can you count on it?

Yep.

So, what are you to do about it? First of all, expecting it to happen is a great step toward handling it especially if you have a plan of reaction and action in place. It's part of that be prepared

Mommy

philosophy we've talked about. I like making tried and true suggestions and leaving you room for making up your mind and using your creativity.

Acting out is the older kid version of a temper tantrum in many ways. It comes in so many forms whether it's lying. defying rules, anger issues, yelling, hitting, talking back disrespectfully, irresponsibility, or non-compliance. They do it for a reason. They do it to aggravate you. It's attention seeking behavior. Your child believes their behavior is justified. It takes concerted effort, but you will be well served to get into their mindset.

Help them help themselves in this very crucial growing up process.

- No matter their age any acting out by your child must be addressed. I know it's easy to let it slide when you're busy with other concerns, or tired, or especially when they get older. A disparaging comment will not get the results you want. Pleading is useless and counterproductive. Ignoring it is like fuel. Address it to stop it.

- Meet it head-on in the moment.

Do not threaten delayed punishment. It is ineffective.

Stop whatever you're doing at the time and correct your child

Acting Out

to stop their behavior. Otherwise, you give them permission to continue and fuel to escalate. Their memory is short. By the time you get around to addressing punishment later, they won't connect the relevance.

- Begging your child to behave is ineffective and worse, it minimizes your position of authority. Yes, I know how tempting to say *please stop. I need you to behave.* I've done it myself in moments of exasperation. We all have from time to time. Make a decision to limit those times to be as few as possible. When you beg and plead you relinquish all power. They've got you.

When my two were about five and four we went to McDonald's for a Happy Meal. (Yes, I have done that. Fast food does have more healthy alternatives since the eighties.) Both kids were restless and wouldn't remain in their seats while we ate. I gave them a warning telling them to sit down or we would leave. Well, you know what happened. They squirmed some more. They needled each other.

Here's what I did.

I stopped talking. I gathered them up, grabbed my purse, and we exited the restaurant leaving our food on the table. I had never done that before. I am an explainer by nature and try to give my little ones reasons why things are what they are but in this case they already knew the score. Both kids were in a bit of a shock and went suddenly quiet. As we loaded into the car, my older one asked

Mommy

why we left. I repeated my request and told her they hadn't done what I asked, and I was following through with the commitment I made. Both remained quiet all the way home.

I never had to leave a restaurant or food on the table again.

The best part of the story is the next time we went to McDonald's, the manager spotted me ordering and came over and told the cashier lunch was complimentary. He told me he had never seen a mom follow through on her threat of punishment for acting out so calmly and effectively. He said removing them but leaving the uneaten lunches on the table amazed him the most. He had repeated the story many times since.

I tell you this story not as a pat on my back but to let you know you have choices other than overreacting or not acting at all. I must say, it was difficult in the moment. I knew I didn't want to plead with them because that's so annoying to overhear in a restaurant. I sure wasn't going to ignore it which is the second most annoying thing you can observe moms do in a restaurant. Yelling, the number one most disturbing mom behavior you can witness wasn't an option.

Every parent knows this territory. People appreciate your efforts.

Your child will get the message when you stay consistent. Any moment of discomfort or embarrassment or inconvenience will seem very small when compared to the results.

Acting Out

Kids test limits sometimes because they feel defiance is their best option, sometimes because the feeling is overwhelming, and sometimes because they don't have the maturity to stop themselves.

A child's greatest desires are to be loved and accepted. Sound familiar? All humans have these as basic needs. You spend your life seeking them. Being seen and heard, having your opinion matter, loving and being loved in return, and having someone care about your feelings are the same desired concepts at any age.

Your child will do *anything* for your attention.

Any of your attention.

That means if you are generous with your praise you will inspire favorable behavior from your child. If the only way your child can get your attention is with unfavorable behavior, they will misbehave in order to get it.

Any reaction, even if that's punishment, is their goal.

Let's face it. Inappropriate behavior *will* get a reaction every time. Acting out is the fastest way to get a mom to turn her attention directly at the offender. It seems counterintuitive to say that a child *wants* to get in trouble, but sometimes trouble is the only choice they think they have.

Mommy

What they really want in that moment is for you to see and hear them.

They want you to choose them over everyone else and anything else in that moment.

I know some kids are more defiant in nature than others. This will throw you a curve if you have an easy child first and expect repeats from the next. Each child will challenge you in some way and this one can be tough.

Remember personality traits are often genetically coded but that doesn't mean a person any age can't make an effort to adjust and to change their behavior. You know as an adult that is often what is required.

A child can learn to make an attitude or emotional style change as well. It takes time and it takes instruction. It takes a lot of patience on your part. You don't have the luxury of giving up. Your child's future behavior depends on how you help them manage their emotions now.

CHAPTER 17
Relationships

You and your baby or toddler feel like you're in your own world much of the time. Part of your mom job is to help them learn about the world outside your door. You get to choose when. It begins with engaging with other people. You get to decide who. Siblings, grandparents, and other family members are their starting place.

It may seem dramatic to say, but this is where your child forms their interpersonal style and social skills, and those relationships shouldn't be taken for granted. It's easy to think these early relationships are a given and they don't require any instruction on your part. That couldn't be further from the truth.

Logic tells you that the love from these people in your child's life is guaranteed, but there should be boundaries and expectations and deal breakers of acceptable behavior in place. Because these close relationships are secure it makes them the safest and best place to learn how to get along with others who don't share in that commitment.

Mommy

Grandparents are the next relationship in line after you and your partner. This relationship is so important because it establishes that familial bond that can be such a support in your child's life. Grandparents offer a perspective from experience that can complement your objectives. The sooner you get the grandparents in your life on board to be that for your child the better. Include them in this celebration at every chance.

Hopefully, you'll have compliant grandparents in your child's life and yours who are sensitive to their needs and your goals.

Stand your ground on the things that matter and learn to cut grandparents slack when they don't quite understand. Again, this is your child and your mommy style, but you will benefit, and your child will benefit from grandparent involvement. If their suggestions or methods are too old-school for you, be open and encourage them to be open to discussion. They might not be as stubborn or as clueless as you might be tempted to think. If they are or if they refuse to cooperate then decide what that means to you.

Grandparents are a permanent component in your child's life whether it is daily interaction or once a year. Your child deserves to know them. They also deserve to form their own relationship with them separate from yours and without any bias you might have. Let them have a relationship that rewards all parties.

- Include grandparents in your child's life.

Relationships

- Make your expectations of grandparents' role clear to them and be open to what they want as well.

- Set clear boundaries of acceptable grandparent behavior. That's a fancy way of saying let them know affection is expected and encouraged but spoiling is not. Be a good leader and make your expectations and deal-breakers known.

- Allow your child to form their own relationship with grandparents. Everyone will benefit.

This is an intense relationship with much room for fulfillment and for disappointment if a balance isn't achieved. I believe grandparents hold much power in creating a foundation not only for your child's life but for your life as well. It's one of the most special connections but it takes insight and self-awareness from mothers and grandparents to ensure it enriches everyone involved.

Siblings

If you have multiple children, then you automatically have sibling rivalry in the mix. Now if you have multiples you may be saying, *oh Becki, you're mistaken because my kids are going to adore each other and be best friends!*

I hope so. I really do.

Mommy

But I know that doesn't automatically happen. In fact, it may not happen at all if you don't take some steps to help set up that possibility for them. You set the tone.

Here are some mommy hacks for siblings I have found will help.

- From day one, make sure the older sibling knows they have not been replaced in anyway. Present the new baby to them as a gift. This is YOUR new baby brother or sister.

- You'll need to institute new rules for your older child's behavior that certainly center around the safety of the new baby. Make these clear but present them as general rules that aren't necessarily pointed at them. Encourage their participation.

- You'll need to establish some rules for your older child about their behavior for your stress management and convenience. These will likely be rules about when the baby is sleeping. Banging drawers, loud toys, yelling, or touching the baby to waken them will become sources for extreme agitation on your part. There's nothing quite as frustrating as getting a cranky baby to sleep only to have a four-year-old slam the bathroom door.

- You'll need to say *not right now* or *wait a minute*, or *I have to take care of the baby first* a hundred times a day. There's no way to be careful every time but when you can say *it's your turn next* or *you get to be first the next time,* you'll help your older child feel

Relationships

less inequity where your time is concerned. It's really as simple as what you say and how you say it. It doesn't require any more of your time or effort just a matter of which words you choose. It can make a world of difference in the older child's behavior and attitude. Make it easier on all of you.

- Make time every day for alone time with the older sibling even if it is only a few minutes. Let that child know you are taking that time specifically for them when the new baby is not included. Now I know you are exhausted, and this sounds like another drain on your energy, but it can be a few minutes of quiet on the sofa together or curled up reading a book of their choice or bath time. Make it a snack-time ritual when the baby's napping to chat about whatever the older sibling wants to talk about. Don't insist on talking about the new baby.

- When your older child acts out because of jealousy be prepared and react with intent. Threats made when your child knows you won't follow through mean nothing. I know it may be difficult to stop and correct one child when your hands are full managing another, but you still have your words. Chose them for instruction, not pleading. Make your demand known.

You can follow through with your consequence with a small delay as long as you are explaining it all the while so that the child's action and the ultimate consequence stay connected in their mind. Remember their memories are short.

Mommy

- Give your older child tasks that involve the caretaking of the new baby but make them seem like a privilege not a punishment or obligation. You'll be amazed what a bit of emotional investment and sense of self-esteem can be accomplished through the confidence building of small tasks. Extra hands will help you.

Start fostering affection between your kids early on. Place value on their mutual companionship and watch them assume it as a practice. Remember they see everything and do what they see.

You are at the head of this train.

Get everyone on board.

CHAPTER 18

Fighting

This chapter is about dispute and conflict resolution.

Whoa, that sounds awfully technical and official for dealing with kids. But isn't that what fighting's all about? There's a dispute over something and the conflict between the people involved must be managed to be resolved.

Conflict resolution is one of the first and most important life skills to learn. The quality of interpersonal relationships depends on how well you manage conflict. Your job as a mom is to equip your child with those tools.

I bet you never thought about handling kids fighting over toys or who gets to go first in the game of Candyland or who gets to hold the new puppy as dispute and conflict management. That's exactly what it is and the same techniques that work for adults work for children. Even small children.

Children need to learn the value of cooperation. It's the way you

Mommy

get your needs and desires met and the way you gain the support of others your entire life. Everything you do that involves someone else is a negotiation. Some are simple and agreed upon almost automatically. Others are major strategic processes.

This starts in your home. How you and your partner handle disputes between yourselves is your child's first example. They see whether reason and logic are used. Whether courtesy and respect are offered.

Kids miss nothing.

They are all-seeing.

I repeat this concept many times. That's because the sooner that settles in your mind the better. It should be a factor in everything you do. You are NEVER off duty as a mom.

They also possess a sixth sense. They're hyper-sensitive to the emotional atmosphere within your walls. They're like a seismic meter of that pressure constantly monitoring for tremors and following the activity on the fault line that may exist.

Know that they know.

You think they're too little to pick up on adult conflict, but they do.

Fighting

They might not comprehend your words, but they can detect your tone. Your choice of words matters. Your tone speaks volumes. Your child may not be able to understand the nuances or even the particulars but what they do sense is the existence of the disruption.

You may look at your newborn and you can't possibly imagine ever being in conflict with them. Cause trouble? Not, that sweet little thing! Or you may have a toddler or even a teen in your life and you can't imagine NOT having conflict be part of your relationship! No is their favorite word.

There are effective ways to manage disputes and conflict between you and your child.

Start with you since that's the most likely place you can initiate progress. Ask yourself some clarity questions.

- Are you being patient? No blame here. Looking for facts.

- Are you making yourself clear? Listen to what you're saying.

- Do you express yourself with age-appropriate words?

- Do you explain and are you calm when you do? Again, think evaluation not judgement. You're trying to investigate here.

Mommy

- Do you mandate and exercise authority without other justification? This is that *because I told you so* time. I know it's easy to say because it's true. You DID tell them probably dozens of times. But it isn't sinking in. Resist saying it at all costs.

  I know your words should be law, but I will ask you to consider the downside to asking your child to accept authority without questioning. It minimizes their feelings and inhibits their recognition of the value of analytical thinking for critical decision making. Most importantly, it can set them up to be vulnerable and susceptible to adults who might use their position of authority to influence them or manipulate them for harm. Your child can learn to respect authority but measure someone's trustworthiness by their behavior if you model that worthy behavior.

- Do you offer equity? That means allowing your child to state their case. Give them a voice. The value of this is two-fold. From your listening they learn that their feelings are valuable. In later relationships throughout their life this will be crucial to their confidence, self-esteem, and happiness. They will require that from others as a deal-breaker in their relationships. It helps them learn to advocate for themselves.

  Then you can use their feelings as a starting place to begin to give them instruction. Reason with them to help them see both sides of the argument. This is their beginning of understanding the need to discern what is reasonable. It's the start of their

Fighting

negotiation skills that will serve them later in their relationships and their career life.

- Teach them the value of listening by listening to them. Once they feel they've been heard they will learn you must also be heard. It's a type of choreography that once they see it repeated, they'll do the steps by rote.

Think of how often you've disagreed with someone whether it was your child, your partner or someone else and you kept wishing they would stop arguing and listen. Time and energy get wasted.

I hear you saying *Becki, are you kidding? I'm supposed to stop in the middle of my child's defiance and reason with them?*

I know perfectly well how unrealistic this may seem. You get tired and your child can have the stubbornness of a pack of mules, but I'm telling you this will pay off in the long run. Will you do it every time?

No.

But if you do it as often as you can, you will be amazed how well it works. Remember, you're making your home more harmonious and giving your child a life skill at the same time. This is where I use the term spoiled. I think you spoil a child by giving in to their

Mommy

demands and allowing them to think their feelings are the only ones that matter.

It's not the tangible things you give them in abundance that causes the spoiling. It's the supposition that they are somehow immune to the rules that everyone else must follow to get along. It's the demand to have their way.

Let me take a moment to talk about something important about this issue. There's a difference in being spoiled and being entitled.

Being spoiled is expecting to always get what you believe you *want*.

Entitlement is expecting to always get what you believe you *deserve*. You want your child to feel they are entitled to be seen, heard, and valued. It's when the belief is that they aren't required to live up to any standard of behavior or that the standards for others don't apply to them that entitlement is undesirable.

I think we get the terms entitled and privileged confused. Privileged is being given opportunities not available to everyone.

Your child's first foray into learning to cooperate is with you. The second is to learn to handle conflict with siblings if they have any. This is a super important issue because it sets the precedent for how your children get along or don't get along with each other throughout their shared childhood.

Fighting

You set it up.

It's in your hands and under your control.

Completely.

Do you want a home filled with squabbling, bickering, screaming, and or major discord? Or do you want a home where when the inevitable disagreements of cohabitation arise, they are handled well?

You get to choose.

Doesn't that sound wonderful?

It may also sound unbelievable to you if you buy into the prevailing belief that all kids fight especially with each other and even more so with their siblings.

I'm here to tell you that's true.

That's because wherever there are two or more people no matter their ages, conflict will arise. What I want to convey to you is that you can limit its scope and effect with intention within your home and between your kids.

Mommy

One of your jobs under the main heading of mom job is head referee.

Rules of engagement must be set in place.

Those rules must be consistent and consistently applied by you.

Also think about how you can influence how often those disagreements between your children occur by your attitude toward them. I will talk about sibling rivalry among older kids in greater detail in the next section. For these youngest ages and phases the fighting tends to be physical. Because very young children are less sophisticated in their anger styles, the issues are usually about personal possession and not wanting to share. Then there's the yelling and physical confrontation that small children do when they fight. This can lead to an unpleasant home atmosphere.

You are in charge of your home. Are you getting that deep down?

Do not relinquish that position because you're too tired to be the compromiser. I know it is exhausting to be a full-time referee. The most expedient antidote is separation. Separate siblings when they're too young to comprehend compromise. Limit the chance for physical confrontation. But take the time to explain your reasoning and to give instruction for what is acceptable or unacceptable behavior. Only through consistent instruction can you get the message across.

Fighting

One of the basics you owe your child is a place of physical safety. You must protect each child. Because they have little, or no impulse control and their default conflict stance is to physically lash out when they are angry or frightened you must do everything to keep them safe from those impulses when you have multiple small children.

I implore you not to subscribe to the, *all siblings fight* method of parenting. As I have agreed, they do all have conflicts, but physical harm should never be a factor.

Whether your young child has siblings or not they will have to learn to cooperate with others. They have cousins, neighbors, peers and will have classmates soon in their life. It is the first time they become aware of the fact that other people have feelings and that those feelings should matter. It's the beginning of their emergence from the self-centeredness of early childhood where their focus is on their own needs and desires to recognizing part of their purpose is to be a part of a community.

It is the birthplace of empathy.

This is crucial to their development into productive citizens and good people.

Again, this has to be given in age-appropriate words and

Mommy

expectations of performance. Adjust those accordingly. Start with elementary concepts and build.

Little kids don't know about the dynamics of conflict. To them, they fuss and fight.

With a very young child begin with validating the fact that your child has feelings and help them manage them for their benefit. I believe the best place to begin to handle conflict at any age is to take a moment to stop and think about the difficult situation so that the response isn't a knee-jerk reaction. With young children especially, the knee-jerk is the only response they know.

To help them begin to learn the concept of anger management and dispute and conflict resolution a.k.a. the impulse to fight, ask your toddler or young child these questions.

- Why are you angry in this moment?

- What does that feel like? Offer your child a suggestion to give their anger a physical shape. They relate well to similes. It feels like____, fill in the blank. It's like asking them to draw a picture with words. Kids are highly receptive to visuals. They live in a show-and-tell world. Play that game with them to teach them cooperation.

- What do you want to happen next?

Fighting

- Is that why you did what you did?

- Did it work?

The next step is to get them to learn to control negative impulses that they may feel.

- Did you hurt the other person physically?

- How did you feel about that? Notice this is what we talked about earlier. Choose your words intentionally. *Instead of asking how the situation made them feel ask how they feel about the situation.* Start early teaching your child that emotions are choices under their control.

- Did the other person hurt you back?

- How do you feel about that? Again, make sure your question isn't how did that make you feel? Give them a sense of control.

- Did you hurt their feelings?

- What do you think that felt like?

- Do you like to feel that way?

- Would you like them to do that to you?

Mommy

Then you must help your child discover ways to make amends. This is a major step in learning cooperation. Ask these questions.

- How do you think the other person feels now after this fight?

- How do you feel about that?

- What can you do now to help them feel better?

- Wouldn't you feel better helping them?

- Will you tell them you're sorry?

Next step is to help them learn from their mistakes. This is a huge step in personal development at any age and you will be giving your child a great head-start by asking these questions.

- How do you feel now?

- Do you want this to happen again?

- What can you do the next time this problem happens?

- Is there something you can think of to do next time instead of fighting?

These questions are the foundation of self-awareness for your child

Fighting

in teaching them the part they play in not only conflict but their ability to manage problems with analytical thinking.

Breaking a problem down into logical steps of progression demonstrates not only their responsibility in but their ability to control the situation.

This is a huge confidence builder.

This also begins a practice of critical thinking that will benefit them as they mature and the problems that they face become larger in scope and more pervasive in consequences.

PART THREE:

FLY, BABY FLY

CHAPTER 19

Leaving The Bubble

These ages and stages we've talked about when your baby grows to be a toddler and approaches becoming a preschooler is the time that I call The Bubble. You get to totally create their environment and the two of you have an opportunity to experience each other without much distraction.

I love being in The Bubble.

It's that memory-making time when the world goes on in its chaotic way outside your door while inside you get to create an insulated life for you and your little one that's controlled and calm. You can "check out" a bit from all the other concerns. It's a time to bond in a connection that only the two of you share. As we've discussed you are in control of the other people you let in during this time.

You've also lived through colic, diaper rash, first colds, teething,

Mommy

vaccinations, bumped heads, learning to walk, talk and feed themselves. There was weening, bedwetting, and giving up the sippy cup. There's no statuette on the mantel but there should be because you're an accomplished potty-trainer. You've survived giving up the pacifier or thumb and watched your tadpole become a fish without floaties. You've giggled until your side hurt and welled with happy tears, built a thousand Lego towers, attended hundreds of tea parties, and watched Sesame Street until you know the neighbors on that street better than yours.

This is a sweet time to be savored and treasured.

You're best buddies. You get each other's jokes, know each other's push-buttons, can finish each other sentences, and sense each other's mood swings.

You get them on their way to independence and then it's time to share them with the rest of the world. They aren't leaving the nest, but they are ready to leave The Bubble. You may be so ready you can hardly wait. Or you might be so reluctant because you can't fathom letting them go even if it's for only a few mornings a week.

It's easy to get so wrapped up in your job that you can't imagine it changing. This is that time almost all moms wish they could freeze their kids and keep them small.

It's the beginning of many times you will be faced with these

Leaving The Bubble

conflicting emotions of being so happy your child is gaining independence and sad that their autonomy means they don't seem to need you.

Going to preschool is one of the first of these autonomy milestones. You can't believe they have grown up and the anticipation for you both is exciting and stressful.

Your first job is to ease your child's fears and concerns without letting yours show. This is the beginning of many times when you will be asked to hold back your emotions so that your child can move forward. Here's what I want you to remember.

These are the moments that you have worked so hard for. These are the moments that you see your child becoming the person you hoped they would be living the life you prayed would happen. Take it in. Hold it close. This is a celebration moment. This is why you do what you do.

So, what does your child stepping out of The Bubble and entering the outside world mean? Up until now you've been the one who has chosen the people around them. Now they have classmates and teachers.

It may be the first time they have been around other children.

Mommy

It may be the first time they have been separated from you.

It may be the first time they have been away from home.

It may be the first time they have taken instruction from another adult not their parent.

Now your job is to ease them into a new environment that may have a different way of working, a different schedule, and maybe different rules. That's a lot for them to handle. Depending on their emotional style the transition may be difficult. Your job now becomes knowing how to champion them when they need it and when and how to help them comply.

- Present going to school as an exciting opportunity. Much like the theory of presenting books and reading as a treat to be treasured, present preschool in the same manner. Remember all they know is what they know. What they know is what you tell them. You are in control of the narrative at this point.

- Allow your child to tell you how they're feeling. This is a critical practice. If begun early, it has a better chance of continuing as your child ages. You will want this line of communication to always be open and available.

- Let your child know you understand their apprehension.

Leaving The Bubble

- Try not to "buy into" the apprehension with too much sympathy or they'll get the upper hand and play on it to stall their compliance.

- Reassure them without pleading with them to cooperate.

- Explain that you have felt this way yourself before. Empathy is a great tool. Explain your worries soon were replaced with fun and it was fine.

- Shame should never be an option.

- Begin early to get the concept of accountability in your child's mind. Going to school is going to be part of their job description as a child. (We'll talk more about that a little later.) The reward of going to school to learn new things needs to be established as their payoff for cooperating.

- Emphasize safety. Your child needs to feel safe with the new people in their life. Assure them that their teacher cares about them and will take care of them. Let them know you trust their teacher.

- Support their teacher. Even if a teacher isn't your favorite one year, pretend to like them. Your child needs to know that you respect their teacher. Remember you're setting them up for school success and the teacher is a major player in your child's

Mommy

happiness during the school day and in their attitude about school in general. One bad year can spell trouble for keeping your child engaged. Your support will help them comply much more readily as they will follow your lead.

- Pick your issues. If they don't want to wear a hair bow to school, don't insist. If they want to wear the same socks every day and it makes them feel confident, then let them. The only person you need to be concerned about is them, not the other mothers in the hook-up line.

My granddaughter had a favorite Hello Kitty T-shirt and a floral cotton skirt she wore to school almost every day the year she was five. She had done fine the two years in preschool prior, but for some reason that year she had separation anxiety and was reluctant to go into class. No matter the weather, no matter the amount of coaxing or attempts at persuasion, she donned that same outfit every morning.

It was like her armor she put on before the battle.

Or maybe it was her security blanket.

Her mother was of course baffled, concerned, worried, frustrated, and a little embarrassed. The other five-year-olds were in their adorable velour sweatshirts and matching pants or their cute leggings in the middle of winter but this kiddo was summer picnic ready.

Leaving The Bubble

But this wise mother didn't let it become an issue. She let go of her feelings and put her child's first. It wasn't hurting her to wear the same outfit. She was hesitant to go into class each morning, but she did. Mommy continued to reassure her child that the teacher loved her, and her friends cared for her and she adored her. This mom knew that being five would come and go, the anxiety would pass, no one would die from embarrassment, and before long it would be a funny story to tell.

All came true. The next year my granddaughter happily retired the favorite and by then much faded Hello Kitty tee, wore a school uniform with no complaints, and sashayed enthusiastically into kindergarten and toward the rest of her school career.

- Be prepared for the school politics that begin as early as preschool. This will be an ongoing theme for the rest of your child's life and yours. I always find that staying in the loop of the classroom and the teacher's agenda is wise. You don't have to be the chairman of the biggest school fundraiser or the head room mother but do stay informed and participate. A little hint here; don't wear yourself out too soon volunteering too much. There really will be many years for you to do all sorts of school activities. Pace yourself!

- Drama can run high in a preschooler's mind. Remember the source before you assume what they are telling you is the complete story. Get the facts before you form an opinion or react.

Mommy

- Don't be blinded by your bias. Being defensive about your child doesn't help if conflict arises. Conversely, be their advocate when needed.

- Remember all of the above because they will serve you for the rest of the school years ahead.

Your child will have classmates that they adore, ones they tolerate, and ones that they do not like. Isn't that pretty much the way you feel about the people you have in your life? Allow them that.

Their classroom is like a work environment where co-workers must co-exist and cooperate. It is a microcosm of different personalities and temperaments and this age they are very immature in their emotional development. Each is representative of different family dynamics and emotional styles. This is probably the first time your child has been exposed to anything other than your way of doing things.

Because they have been learning by your expectations and within your boundaries of what is acceptable and what is unacceptable, they will likely have a hard time understanding when another child acts differently. Your child may even present as the authority-figure student who feels the need to correct others when they don't follow the rules your child knows. Encourage their leadership but temper it with some people skills! Help them to channel their inner boss in a positive direction. This will be a great life skill later on.

Leaving The Bubble

Preschool is the first place outside your home that your child will practice their citizenship. This is where interpersonal skills will begin to shape how others view them. This is where what you have already taught them about conflict management comes in and pays off. When they are confronted by a classmate, they will have the skills in place to handle it without getting physical.

Let me say here that part of your job in dispute and conflict management is to make sure your child can defend themselves when appropriate. This means they must learn to advocate for themselves. They have to learn to defend and stand up for themselves and to be confident in the face of conflict. That's a fine line you will have to help them distinguish with each incident. Use whatever comes up as a teachable moment.

Being a self-advocate also means learning the value of compromise. That's very different than submission. It's also very different from bullying.

Hopefully your child has already learned the difference between a mutual disagreement and bullying. Talking about bullying with your child provides them with the tools to recognize the difference and to know it is ALWAYS unacceptable to bully someone or to be bullied. Having that knowledge will empower them to stand up for themselves and for others.

Preschool is also where you will first become hyper-aware of the

Mommy

parenting styles of the parents of your child's friends. You may assume that all parents of a four-year old have pretty much the same parenting views and methods. These folks are usually your peers and most likely in the same socio-economic group.

You'll come to find that isn't always the case.

Some of the other parents will become your mom buddies and you'll love sharing the school experience with them. If you're lucky you'll find one or two that you really identify with and most importantly you agree with their parenting practices and style.

You will also learn that families can differ vastly. This is the beginning of your experience with how the legacy of others influences your child's relationships. There're all those things we have already talked about core values, conflict management, discipline, rituals like mealtime and manners, boundaries, and expectations all become fertile ground for contrasts in family dynamics. You will spend time explaining why you feel differently than so-and-so's mom and why certain behavior that she allows isn't allowed by you.

Do it in a way that explains your reasoning without condemning if possible. There are two reasons I advise this. One is it reinforces showing acceptance of others' values with genuine empathy and two is because kids repeat everything they hear. Chances are pretty high your child will tell the other one what you said. Save yourself from hearing your words come back at you by an insulted parent.

Leaving The Bubble

Think about all of this as really positive news. You're helping shape a future stellar student and someone who will be a good friend to others. Someone who can be open-minded while they retain their own set of values.

See how much you are doing for the world?

And you thought you were simply delivering your preschooler to class without a meltdown!

This is the beginning of what I call *mommy magic*. Your innate ability to know what is best even when you might doubt yourself.

Trust your gut.

Your child will count on it.

CHAPTER 20

Feels Like You've Got This!

Look at you!

You've brought another human safely into the world and gotten them successfully out into the world. You're the mom of a certified grade schooler.

This is another huge milestone for both of you.

For the next few years one grade will seem a lot like the one before and you have a few struggles with getting along with a certain classmate or teacher, but for the most part, you've got this.

The elementary school years can feel like smooth sailing most of the time. You've gotten your child self-sufficient. They sleep by themselves, bath themselves, dress themselves, and feed themselves. They can do their homework, and pick up their dirty clothes, and remember their book report is due tomorrow all by themselves if you let them and more importantly if you expect it of them. They've learned your rules and know your boundaries.

They've learned that there's more to the world than home and that outside space is a big place. They go to school and have gotten the hang of its rules and structure. They've learned some responsibilities for functioning outside your bubble like being ready on time, showing up, managing their time with schoolwork, their friends, and sports.

You're making decisions about which TV shows and movies they watch, safe computer practices, screen time, social media, and cell phones.

Caution is not overprotection.

Overprotection is what the word implies. It's too much, overkill, excessive and unnecessary. Caution is good wariness. It's thoughtful consideration of all the factors.

It's tempting to want to shelter your child especially the firstborn because you don't have experience with trusting your judgement on these outside influences and you don't have the luxury of the proven results of your judgment. It's so easy to question yourself especially if you have experts, your mother, your friends, your child all telling you what to do. You may even face criticism.

Feels Like You've Got This!

Your child won't be warped, and you won't expire because you withstood the protests and you said no.

Some of your child's needs will change as they age. You will need to be aware and in tune with the subtle ways kids communicate sometimes, especially when they aren't sure what to do with feelings they may not understand or recognize.

It is very easy to dismiss the depth of those emotions because you know from being a child yourself once that things that feel drastic to a child will pass with time.

All kids go through this you'll say and it's true. The thing to remember is that each child goes through it differently because each is a unique individual. Allow them that latitude.

Tap into them emotionally. This is where your human empathy can aid you as a mom. Remember what it's like to be a kid in a grown-up world.

Elementary school is one of those times. They're dealing with the outside world and home is their safe place. They may have trouble at school getting the teacher's attention or being included in friendships and activities. They face rejection without having the skills or the perspective to handle it. They're searching for acceptance. They need yours. They need your affirmation that their feelings are valid.

Mommy

The world isn't fair. You're going to have to help them accept that while inspiring them to seek to change that.

I believe every child has a job just like you have a mom job. The description of their job is to do well in school and be a good person. That's really all you're asking them to do. School is important because it's so much of their life from ages six to eighteen. It's the foundation of so much of their future in terms of options and opportunities. Being a good and decent person is all we can ask of anyone because it's so all encompassing. This is where all those life skills you're giving them come in and where the quality of their life mirrors the quality of their character. All the other things pale by comparison.

CHAPTER 21

Sibling Rivalry

You might have rocked your world and your firstborn's world in a big way. It was a great decision for your family and one that you have every right and reason to make if you choose. But it changes things.

In fact, it changes *everything*.

Your family might have welcomed a new sibling or two into your universe. It may have gone fairly easily, or it may have been a major deal with your firstborn. We touched on this earlier when we talked about little ones. With time you work out the kinks of having rules about the dos and don'ts of playing, sharing, bathing, and age-appropriate cooperation. You expect some resistance, and it happens. Kids get over it. How well they get over it and how it affects their ongoing relationship with each other and with you in this regard is dependent on how you handle it.

As your kids get older this may be the bumpy part so let's talk about that. This goes back to the idea of conflict management and setting boundaries for behavior. It also is an issue rooted in your child's self-esteem.

A sibling IS competition.

Period.

No way around it.

There's only one of you.

Now there are two or more of them.

The push-button spot for all kids with siblings is in vying for their mom's attention. This is partly because they have that competition. That competition isn't going anywhere. Also, the older ones often find themselves needing that attention more once outside influences are a source of conflict for them. If someone is being mean or they feel left out at school, they will seek your attention and be more resentful of a sibling if they feel they are in their way of receiving it.

How can you help them? How can you minimize the impact of sibling rivalry?

Let's go back over a couple of things we've talked about. Each of your children is different form the other. Like any two people

Sibling Rivalry

in the world, they have very separate personalities and different temperaments.

Ask yourself these questions and consider these options to help your kids get along with each other for your happier household. Remember, you're the head referee. See yourself sporting that cool black baseball cap, turning up the collar on that snappy black and white stripe shirt, and sporting that shiny whistle on a chain around your neck when it's referee time.

- Do you recognize that your kids are not clones? One child's emotional style can differ widely from the other. One size does not fit all.

- *Give them room to be individuals.*

- Do you subscribe to the "*all siblings fight*" theory? How about the "*kids will be kids*" theory? You're better than that kind of thinking and so is your child.

- *Kids will rise or fall to your expectations.*

- Is your referee style one of fairness? Do you favor one child over the other in disputes? Please be aware that your kids know when you have favorites, and they will use it against each other. I urge you not to give them this ammunition.

Mommy

- **Have favorite things about each child but don't favor one child over the other.**

- Are your expectations of how your child handles conflict age-appropriate? The ages of your kids and the number of years between their ages are huge factors.

- Please resist the urge to compare your children to each other in front of each other.

- **Labels that are emotionally charged are non-removable.**

- Even if you try to take it back the imprint remains. You will set it up so that your children are in constant conflict if you say one is the good one or the easy one while labeling the other the troublemaker. All those hideous labels of lazy, not intelligent, hard-headed, hot-headed, and the like are so damaging anyway, but when used to describe one child in a moment of comparison to a sibling who is opposite can be devastating.

- **Engage and enlist the older ones in the process of conflict management by giving them an investment in the resolution.**

- If they feel more in control of the outcome, they will be more

Sibling Rivalry

vested in the process of reconciliation. But do it in a way that puts the responsibility on them not the spotlight where the other child feels defensive and resentful of the other child.

- *Consistency, consistency, consistency.*

- It's hard to take the time in the moment every time to resolve the conflict but it's worth it.

- Maintain the ritual of taking time for each child. In the same way you're little one needed reassurance they are still loved, your elementary schooler needs that security. Being bigger and older doesn't equate to smaller feelings or needs. In fact, those emotions become much larger. Even if it's only for a few minutes, take time for each child separately to focus on them alone. Make sure they know you're doing it intentionally for them.

- *In elementary school a child's emotions are gargantuan compared to their physical size. Remember that.*

- Stick with your commitment to make bullying a major rule violation with consistent monitoring and reinforcement. Bullies get their start at home. No one is born a bully. It is a learned behavior. Since your home is their only environment, the only way your child learns bullying behavior is by your example and or your acceptance of that sort of behavior from them.

Mommy

Bullying between siblings is never okay. Please do not allow one of your children to bully the other for any reason. This is the breeding ground of the misconception that someone can mistreat another person with intimidation and humiliation for ANY reason. Ever.

You owe your child a place of emotional safety as well as physical safety.

- *Teasing is a form of bullying.* I know that may sound a bit extreme, but teasing is the gateway to the same vein of humiliation. It's about causing some degree of emotional discomfort for another person and getting some sort of reward from it usually some form of personal satisfaction. Think about that for a moment. There's a big difference between laughing *with* a child about something they do and laughing *at* them. Older siblings can be led to believe they can get away with teasing because it's *only* their sister or their brother as if they don't count. This sets up room for conflict and lasting jealousy unnecessarily. Each child's self-esteem is fragile and especially with those closest to them. Set an example by not engaging in any sort of teasing and not tolerating it.

Birth order has been studied for years. There are patterns that emerge, and commonalities exist. Then there are the exceptions. One thing is for sure. Every firstborn has an advantage of being the only child a mom has to focus on at the time. They benefit from

Sibling Rivalry

the singular attention but bear the brunt of the trial-and- error process. You have more time to teach a firstborn and more time to play, read, talk to, play with, and focus on them. You have more time to rest when they rest.

You expect much of the one to whom you give so much.

Then you dethrone them with a new object of your affection. I have observed that this is more often met with their acceptance as they have already begun to believe they are as fabulous as you've been telling them they are! Firstborns do seem to possess a strong sense of confidence. But again, every child is different so don't assume because they are the oldest a child will be a certain personality type.

When another sibling comes along the oldest is expected to learn the completely unfamiliar concept of sharing.

Second children tend to be pleasers mainly because they never know a time they're not in competition and the fastest way to "win" a mom's affection is to be compliant. Who doesn't love someone who does what they are asked and offers to do more? What mom doesn't appreciate a child who picks up the slack and helps in any way? When the oldest is already the star, the next child usually find the best way to be recognized is by being low maintenance. If the second becomes sandwiched between the older and a younger, then they can often find themselves the peacemaker of the family again because it garners the most reward by comparison.

The youngest child has the advantage and disadvantage of parents who are a bit weary of the grind. You're pretty unphased at the antics, aware of the tactics, and more relaxed about the process. It's easy to let that familiarity to translate to complacency. Your vigilance wanes and you can be tempted to give in to their wiles. The idea that all youngest children are spoiled is a self-fulfilling prophecy you alone as the mom control. Your partner, the grandparents, and others may be inclined to favor this child with leniency. You are the arbiter of the outcome. No child is born spoiled or given the privilege by anyone else but you.

ALERT: This is a big burden I'm about to lay on you. Before I tell you what it is, I'm going to tell you the upside that you can use to your advantage. Remember it as you read on.

Whether your children get along with each other is totally in your hands. They may butt heads figuratively, but you control whether they act on it.

Okay, I hear what you're saying, and I see you shaking your head in response to that. You're saying, *if only that were true*.

Sibling Rivalry

Think for a moment how fabulous it would be to have everyone get along most of the time.

Now think about how fabulous you'd feel if you had that ability.

You do.

If you are doing this effectively, YOU are in charge of your home, your kids are not. Create and insist on the environment you want.

I know that's another part of the job that's a huge responsibility and a huge pain to keep in mind and keep on top of constantly. Think about it. You set the tone for civility. You decide what's acceptable and unacceptable. You're in charge of the deal-breakers. You're the disciplinarian with the authority to give rewards and to take away privileges.

Here's where you will also need to be cognizant of each child's individual needs. Their personality may need constant reassurance. They may be the opposite and things roll off their back. They may be the more difficult to discern type and you have to monitor what they need because it changes. Some will feel the rivalry deeper than others. You'll have to determine.

If you want your children to be friends now and later in life, make it a priority to cultivate their cooperation. Give them the chance to discover each other's strengths, honor each other and protect each other by demonstrating your willingness to do so and to reward their support. Encourage them to see their siblings as their allies.

A brother or sister can be and should be a gift in life. To have someone who shares your fabric and knows your story like no one else in the entire world. Another living breathing human who knows you intimately and still loves you. Someone who accepts you without question and champions you without reservation is priceless.

You as their mom hold the key to what their shared experience will be. Do you want them to be fellow soldiers on the same battlefield or companions on their journey?

Here's a thought for you that may give you a bit of a jolt for a second. These are the people you are grooming to be the ones who will care for you one day. They will collectively be the ones who decide your aging issues. Now, I get that is a downer thought to you if you're young, but life is a beautiful series of rhythmic events and time flows and carries you forward and there is a natural order of things. Your children forming a circle of love to support one another and you can be one of those life events.

You hold the key.

CHAPTER 22

Tweener Limbo

There comes a time in every child's life where they get waylaid on their destination to being a teenager. They are too old to get away with little kid stuff and too young to begin enjoying the perks of being a teen.

This is the awkward phase I call Tweener Limbo.

Up until now most kids are on the same maturity track and seem fairly alike when compared to their peers. Then nature creeps in and begins to mess with their bodies and their emotions. They may have physical growth spurts and certainly emotional ones where they are nearly infantile one minute and quite grown-up the next.

If you think you're confused, then think about how bewildered they must be.

Hormones are tricky and powerful. They surge and retreat without much warning and just as suddenly they level out. This is go-with-the-flow time if there ever was. You've had this happen to you in your adult life. The difference is you know about hormones and their effects. Your child has no reference or intellectual understanding of them.

Be merciful.

Cut your child some slack on this one.

Your compassion will be rewarded.

Watch your child for cues. Try to stay tuned into what is being said and not said to get a direction for what they need. It's easy to again say this is just a phase. Do everything you can to make sure that's all it is and that your child transitions into their teens as easily as possible.

This is where you make decisions about changing rules. Your tweener will need new ones as they move forward. So, will you. They'll notice and be grateful for your flexibility. You can also use easing rules as an incentive for compliance for adding other responsibilities and privileges. Besides an upgrade on movie ratings and TV shows where is there room for rule adaptation while they are still young? Let's talk about changing the rules.

- Bedtimes and curfews can start with very small increments. Even clothes choices can be utilized as rewards for cooperation. Tweeners have been under the same restrictions throughout

Tweener Limbo

grade school so any adjustment in their favor is seen by them as a big deal. Milk it! This is what I call mom currency. It's based on a barter system of *you do this and I'll do that*. Rather than manipulation or machination this is true reciprocity. Give this to get that and everyone feels the benefit.

- Let your child be in on the conversation. That means decide what adjustments you are willing to make then sit down with them for a discussion. Ask for their input. This doesn't mean you are asking for their opinion. There's a big difference. What your child is seeking as a tween is to be seen, heard, and counted. Can you relate? See, they aren't from another planet after all. Stand next to them on that common ground and let them know you're right there with them.

  Let them feel like they have a voice. This also means listen to that voice. This isn't a set-up situation where you control the narrative. They may surprise you in the innovative things they think of to barter and they may astound you with their self-awareness and maturity. It does happen!

- This one may seem counterintuitive but hang with me here. Try choosing a responsibility they are performing now that can be either removed from their to do list or delegated to a younger sibling. There is great value in earned freedom. It teaches your child that good behavior and dependability pay off. This could be a simple household chore passed to another like feeding the dog or taking out the trash. Simple stuff for great return.

- Add responsibilities that they are now old enough to handle but present them in a way that says they have *earned* it. When they think it's a sign of getting older, they will receive it as a plus on their list. It's also a subliminal way to ease them into the understanding that with age comes more responsibility.

Here's another reality check. Childhood isn't measured only in chronological years, which grade they are in at school, and height markings on the kitchen doorframe.

To your child their life is one big scorecard. What they get to do, where they get to go, who they get to be friends with, which team they get to be on for sports and how much they get to play, how many times they get what they want whether that's an experience or a material item, how many times they get in trouble, how much their sibling gets away with, and on and on.

Notice the word *get* is in each of those things listed. A child has very little control over much of their life. You determine most of it as do other authority figures in their life. Even their efforts of working hard and doing what is expected doesn't always get recognized.

They tend to use gaining control as the scoring system. Even though gaining more freedom as they age means taking on more

Tweener Limbo

responsibilities, it still feels like they are winning the game of childhood.

Win-win, anybody?

It's often difficult for moms to yield to a child's need for privacy. This is a slippery slope where vigilance for their physical safety and their emotional well-being must be traversed carefully. Especially as they grow up.

Watching for clues of any sort of trouble you feel your child may succumb to is imperative. It is one of your number one jobs as they grow older and further away from your line of vision. Red flags should not be ignored. You don't have the luxury of not noticing when the signs are there. Sometimes kids are really proficient at hiding things, but more often than not, they don't have the reasoning power or the discipline to do it well all the time. That's why your job is to stay ever watchful while you slowly give them space.

In this middle ground they're still reliant on you for transportation and permission to participate. That means they may also depend on you to be the arbiter of issues that overwhelm them or where they feel discomfort.

I can't because My mom said no and *because my mom will kill me*

Mommy

are invaluable excuses out of potentially trouble situations your child can count on.

Tweeners are often very social animals. Once they're old enough to have sleepovers and group parties they begin to venture out into unknown territory. This is when they discover that other families don't always operate like yours does. Remember up until now all they know is what they know and that's been limited to your family's way of functioning. Once they get into the homes of their peers it's like a new level of a video game with new players and action. That change of environment coupled with putting them into a herd situation where they are trying to fit in and be noticed while simultaneously wishing to fly under the radar, doubles down on the likelihood of some sort of drama from time to time.

You may recognize it a mile off.

You may never see it coming

I had an agreement with my kids as tweeners. As they began to broaden their circle and the landscape changed, I made a pact with them. If they ever felt uncomfortable in any way with anybody or anything anyplace at any hour all they had to do was call me.

If they called me, I would come immediately to pick them up and bring them home.

Tweener Limbo

Now this next part of my offer is crucial to the success of this practice.

I made a promise.

Call me and I will come get you immediately and –

I WILL NOT ASK YOU ANY QUESTIONS.

Okay, I heard you say *whaaaaaaattttt???*

I know you're thinking *that's too hard*. How can you not ask them what the hell happened to make them want to come home probably in the middle of the night?

Here's where that trust thing comes into play.

Your tweener needs to be able to count on you when they can't count on themselves.

They need to know you'll come to the rescue when they don't feel confident or strong enough to save themselves.

Assure them any way you can and show them you trust them to do this when they don't know what else to do.

Mommy

Here's another issue that you'll face as a tweener mom. I have spent more time explaining the behavior of adults to my children than explaining the behavior of their peers. The parents of your child's friends may parent very differently than you. This will be getting more and more evident with each stage and age.

Or some parents may be bullies to each other, to other parents, coaches or teachers or encourage their kids to be jerks to other kids. Other parents may not have the same value system for themselves or their children. That requires a lot of vigilance on your part and a willingness to stand your ground in a way that registers with your child as good judgement not judgmental.

This tweener place is also filled with all sorts of other issues. School has been pretty much the same for all kids up until now and with only a few exceptions is an even playing field.

Once middle school becomes their location your child will start to find ways to fit in and by a unique kind of natural selection they will begin to separate from the pack in academics, sports, and the performing and visual arts. There are teams to make, parts to get, awards to receive. That means there are teams not made, parts not gotten, awards not won.

It seems someone's always winning and someone's always losing.

Those places of setback can be trips on the sidewalk, stumbles

Tweener Limbo

over the bumps, or summersaults over the cliff to a tweener. Remember they're beginning to shift to the supersize portion of emotional measure. There are no mole hills on this landscape, only mountains and the fumbles and tumbles are like landmines hidden where you least expect them. Things easily explode and implode. There's so much going on and so many personalities involved that your tweener can fall in-between the cracks and be overlooked. So much of who'll they'll become springs from this time that it's easy to dismiss all of the goings on as just middle school.

How you handle defeat or failure to achieve is crucial to how your child perceives the importance and the impact of those concepts and your child's resilience to and recovery from disappointment. It will carry them through the rough spots now and lay a foundation of emotional strength for the difficulties and disappointments of the future. We all have them. Those who are prepared to handle them survive them best.

Let me say here that there will be times YOU will be disappointed when your child doesn't make the team or didn't get the lead in the play.

KEEP IT TO YOURSELF.

Your emotions shouldn't be baggage for your child to carry.

Mommy

Your disappointment magnifies theirs and doubles their guilt for not achieving their desires and goals.

They feel like they've let you down.

Always be ready to lift them up.

PART FOUR:

TEENAGERS

CHAPTER 23

Invasion of the Body Snatchers!

What happened? Where did your baby go? Who is this person sleeping in your house, eating your food, and using your hair products?

Seriously, this is a shock to the system. One day you are looking into the innocent eyes of a toddler or into the face of a wide-eyed grade schooler or at the indignant eye-rolling of a tween.

Now it's into the eyes of someone who is becoming a fully realized person. They've grown so much you might have to look up to make eye contact! And this person is totally self-sufficient in all the physical ways.

They have or will have a driver's license!

Dear God.

Mommy

That means they'll be totally and independently mobile. That also means that the circle of their world now has a much larger radius and encompasses further reaching variables.

The dangers in their life are much the same as before but compounded now by circumstances often of their own making because of the chances of an error in judgement.

You depend on a teen to make grown-up decisions with a teen-aged under-developed brain. The missteps can be damaging, and the mistakes have perilous potential.

Wow, right?

Okay. Breath. I've got some help for you.

Let's start with the basics. Crossing that giant line of demarcation between tweener and teen is a major step. They look different, sound different, may be even smell different! They are more focused on their appearance and their need to conform becomes paramount. They sometimes assume a zombie-like mindset and follow the lead of whichever fellow zombie is shuffling in front of them.

It's like they have no mind of their own.

Invasion of the Body Snatchers!

Where you once wished they weren't so single-minded and head-strong now you just wish they used the brain they've got.

One of my daughters had a group of friends that I nicknamed The Herd. There were thirteen girls that went everywhere together. I was always telling them that individually they were each very intelligent, resourceful girls but when they got together as one group there wasn't a brain between them.

That was of course an exaggeration meant to get the point across to them that their group had a tendency to act much more on impulse and suggestion than they did when they were each alone. We know from the studies of crowd psychology that a group of people has a different dynamic than the individuals in the group.

There are varying theories about why behavior changes or shifts when an individual becomes part of a group and their individual sensibilities adopt the collective self and behaviors. You've heard of crowds acting in counterintuitive ways. That doesn't mean it will be negative participation, but it does mean there is a major force of prevailing influence that comes into play.

Now if that's true of adults with very established principles then you can imagine how vulnerable that makes a teenager who's still forming their moral core.

A teenager's biggest concern is peer acceptance.

Mommy

Their fear is real. They want desperately to fit in by not standing out in any way. You on the other hand are eager for them to perform in ways, especially at school, where they do stand out and receive recognition.

Let's talk a bit about you in this moment. This first teenage birthday will probably hit you with the same sort of emotional response you had the first day you dropped them off at preschool. The world outside your bubble felt too big and too ominous for either of you to take on. But you did slowly as time went on and you moved forward conquering fears and navigating the bumps in the road.

That doorframe where you mark their growth has a dozen or more pen lines with age and height notations by now.

And you have a million memories to match scribbled across your heart.

You have been in authority and now that authority can be seriously challenged.

They want freedom and you want control.

Here you are, the mother of a teenager.

I'm going to ask you to do something. I want you to read the next section and pretend you're a teenager reading about yourself. It's

Invasion of the Body Snatchers!

as if someone slipped into your head and wrote your thoughts. You might think this is a breeze, after all you were a teenager once.

You know what it was like to be a teenager *when you were a teen*.

You have no idea what it feels like to be one today.

You can't.

As times change with each generation so do the issues. And concerns. And pitfalls. That's why I'm devoting an entire section to this phase of life. It is the last time in your mom-child relationship that you will have this much impact at your discretion in your charge.

So, think of the problems you faced and then dump all the modern stuff on top and that's the load your child is carrying right now.

Read this next section as if you were a teen and try to feel the emotions.

Mommy

These are the best years of your life

Are you kidding me?

You're a teenager. Everybody keeps telling you how fun this is supposed to be.

You want to tell them that this is what you imagine as hell.

You feel like you have no control.

The adults in your life are so busy telling you what to do that they don't see the irony of always telling you to use your head and think for yourself.

They want you to be independent, but they won't cut you any slack or allow you any freedom.

They want to choose your clothes, your entertainment, and your friends. And now they have begun telling you what you should do with the rest of your life.

You're just trying to survive middle and high school.

Everything in your life is changing without your permission. Your

Invasion of the Body Snatchers!

body, your mind, your emotions are all over the place, but they feel as though they're working together against you.

Your friends are changing, too. Some of them don't even seem like the same person you knew and they're making decisions that you find conflicting with what you know is right and wrong.

You don't know who to trust.

Then there are your parents. Your dad keeps using sports metaphors to give you advice and your mom posts sticky note affirmations she found on Pinterest all over your mirror.

They're trying too hard.

It's irritating.

Then they put you under a microscope and magnify everything you do and what you say. They ask so many questions so that you feel like they're probing you brain. You know they mean well but you're feeling sick about it.

Then they have the nerve to keep telling you these are the best years of your life. Do they have any idea how ridiculous that sounds? Can't they see you're miserable most of the time? If these are the best of times, then does that mean it doesn't ever get better than this?

Mommy

No wonder you don't want to get out of bed most days.

No wonder you stay perpetually pissed off.

You're happy and you're sad. Your excited about something then you couldn't care less. You're like Dr. Jekyll and Mr. Hyde on steroids and you can't seem to help it. Your brain hurts from the thoughts banging into each other.

Then there's the big stuff. Gender identity and sexual orientation, school requirements, parental expectations, social media chaos, and everyone asking you what you'll major in when you get to college or what you want to be when you grow up.

You couldn't wait to be teenager and now you just want to be a kid again.

Better yet, you want to be left alone.

Then again, the problem is you feel so alone.

You're confused much of the time.

There's too much to remember.

Too many ways to screw up.

Invasion of the Body Snatchers!

But you constantly feel like the one who's getting screwed.

Everything around you exists as some form of cautionary tale. Don't give out any personal information online, don't talk to strangers, don't smoke, don't vape, don't do drugs, don't have sex, don't drink, don't waste time, don't daydream your life away, don't, don't, don't.

Your parents are always trying to scare the sh*t out of you to get you to comply.

Then there are all the dos on your list. Do well in school, do your homework, do your chores, do the right thing, do your best, do everything to make your parents proud.

When you do have something go your way your parents want to make such a big deal about it. Praise feels more like pressure. Do it again. Do it better. Then do it again. Pick something and be the best. Get a scholarship. It takes four years to get through high school and they're all focused on college. They won't let you enjoy this supposed best time of your life ever because all they talk about is the future. They keep trying to put you in a box that looks good and then tell you to think outside of the box.

You know at any minute your life can change. Someone decides to trash you online, your best friend tells everyone else something you said in confidence, your boyfriend/girlfriend cheats on you,

Mommy

your teacher decides to pick on you, you flunk that huge exam, and all hell breaks loose.

At any moment all hell could break loose.

And that's just the friends and school stuff.

Then there might be all the home stuff like your parents constant fighting, alcohol or drug use or abuse, physical and or emotional abuse, divorce and custody battles, dual households, dual families and sets of siblings, money problems, physical illness, mental illness, self-harm. You might be struggling with the death of your parent or sibling.

That's a lot of issues. Most of them depend on the behavior of others in order to get better. The adults keep saying it's time for you to take charge of your life, but they don't allow that to happen with their agendas in play. How can they tell you to get your sh*t together when they are all over the place?

All a constant reminder that you're in a holding pattern until you are old enough to make your own way.

You wish you had a voice.

You wish someone really wanted to listen to what you have to

Invasion of the Body Snatchers!

say. You wish you didn't feel like you need to say what they want to hear.

You really wish you didn't have to talk at all and answer all the ridiculous questions.

Then there's the constant comparison. You're always comparing your life to someone else's or someone else is comparing it to theirs and it seems you're on the short end. Clothes, cars, your looks, vacations, friends, grades, everything is subject to judgement.

It's never enough.

You're never enough.

Pretty much everything sucks.

CHAPTER 24

Same Partner, Different Dance

Reading how a teenager feels and reminding yourself how tough it really is makes you think doesn't it?

You'd trade this stuff for the terrible twos all day long.

You think your teenager isn't thinking at all because most the times you ask them questions the answer is the same.

I don't know.

How do you continue to make sure they become those happy shiny people you imagined when you first stared at them in their crib all those years ago?

Where do you start to get though it?

It begins with an unbreakable, immoveable commitment to your mom job.

You ease where you can and clamp down when their physical safety and or emotional wellness and all those variables are concerned. Here's the key to doing this with the least amount of strife for you and your teenager.

Decide what matters. Make it clear. Follow through.

Remember these basics we've covered.

- Be clear in your expectations. First with yourself and then with them.

- Start sure and strong and your child will follow. What you do for yourself to be a strong mom you give to them.

- Have an action plan in place. Don't make it up as you go or as the situation arises. Ask yourself questions before they become issues. Have your answers set in your mind to keep clarity foremost.

- Kids need consistency from the beginning and all the way through. They don't react well to surprises. They don't have a clue why they do what they do or feel what they feel much of

Same Partner, Different Dance

the time, so they rely on you to have the answers. They can't trust themselves, so they need to count on you to protect them from themselves sometimes.

I will tell you a story from my own mom playbook.

Every mom of a teen has a story like this. It happens. You did it in some variation to your mom. It will happen to you when your child is a teen. You will have to decide how to handle it. This worked for me.

When my kids were teens, I didn't have the wonderful GPS devices or trackers that are available now to assist moms in knowing your child's whereabouts at all times. Mothers relied on our kids to tell us things to keep us informed of their plans and whereabouts.

I didn't have parental supervision when I was an adolescent. My father was chronically ill, and my mom was preoccupied with his care. She physically wasn't around much. I know the dangers of having no parental safety net. That's why I was a hyper-vigilant parent.

We all know what teens can get into and the choices they have to make. You know the things you did that your parents wouldn't have approved of so that's why when you become a parent you get that pang in your gut thinking about the possibilities.

Mommy

When my kids turned thirteen and began to really participate in what I called "herd activities" where they went in groups together to the mall or the movies or to sleep-overs and parties, I laid down a new teenager mandate.

Actually, I presented it more like a law of nature not to be questioned because it was certain and dependable as gravity.

The Law of Track Down

You are now officially a teenager. With this distinction comes all the rights and privileges of my trust. I am trusting you to be WHERE you tell me you are going and with WHOM you tell me you are going with. If I find out you have not told me the truth, I WILL HUNT YOU DOWN and I WILL FIND YOU. And I WILL put you in my car in front of everyone and bring you home. Trust me.

Think I was kidding?

I had to exercise the law only once for one fourteen-year-old. She left our home one evening going to a sleepover with one of her buddies like she had done countless times before. It was such a regular occurrence I didn't think twice about it. A few hours later

Same Partner, Different Dance

another friend's mom called to say she would be late the next morning picking her daughter up from our house. It only took a few seconds to realize chances were pretty good we had both been hoodwinked. I then called the home of the supposed sleepover and asked that mom to call my daughter to the phone because I needed to tell her something. She then told me my daughter wasn't there and her daughter wasn't home because she was sleeping over at one of the other girls' houses.

Quickly I realized we all had been scammed by a handful of crafty teens.

You can imagine what I did next.

Yep.

I did it.

I got in my car and began perusing the neighborhoods where I thought the girls might be. After a while I came to a street where there were probably a hundred teens flowing in and out of a house and crawling over the manicured lawn. The front door of the house was wide open. I recognized it as the home of a couple that I knew well whose son was in my daughter's class at school.

I also knew the parents were away on an overseas trip.

Mommy

Instantly, I knew I had stumbled upon the scene of a my-parents-are-out-of-town teenage party. As I pulled up into the drive, the sea of revelers parted, and someone recognized my car. I heard them shout my daughter's name into the crowd. I parked, sat quietly, and waited. She appeared at the open doorway and walked quickly down the long sidewalk and driveway to my car. Everyone stopped and stared.

I said nothing.

She got into the car and we drove away.

The ride home was silent. I knew I had made my point. She knew what she had done. I had followed through and kept my promise.

I never had to do it again.

Now, I'm not saying she never did anything else I wouldn't have liked or even approved of ever again. I'm savvy enough to know as she got older, she got better at getting away with things. However, I assure you she thought long and hard about situations and there were many she didn't participate in for fear of being caught. That was my intent. I wanted her to think before she acted. Anything I could do to save her from any misstep was my goal. She knew she could depend on my commitment to follow through.

Remember the mantra.

Same Partner, Different Dance

Consistency and follow through.

Here's another one.

Say what you mean and mean what you say.

And then get ready.

Be prepared to perform in punishment and in praise.

Your teen needs to be certain what to expect of you and themselves. The whole world seems random and unreasonable to them. They can't get their bearings most of the time.

You need to be their rock.

Their lighthouse.

Their moor.

Their signpost.

Their level.

Their north star.

Mommy

They need to trust your behavior especially when they can't trust their peers or themselves to be prudent and think things through.

As I mentioned with tweeners, you will really begin to see the differences in how parents choose to parent as your child becomes a teenager. People have a wide range of ideas about what teens should be allowed to do. Some of these in other families may conflict with your beliefs. Drinking, smoking pot, curfews, dating, the list is endless of the ways this may show up.

All I can say is trust your gut again. Stand your ground on the issues that matter to you.

I have seen parents act out and say things they shouldn't have or conduct themselves in ways I found unacceptable, and I have had to make my opinion known so that my kids understood my boundaries. Kids need to know adults can be wrong. That their behavior can be inappropriate.

Now let's talk about talking to your teen.

Lay the groundwork to be heard.

This is crucial.

You are going to be tempted to pull rank. Understood.

Same Partner, Different Dance

You're going to be tempted to declare rather than discuss. I get it.

Remember like in all relationships, communication is key. Negotiation is imperative.

You can't open a dialogue with a closed mind.

Yours or theirs.

You get what you give.

I'm going to repeat the same themes from earlier stages and ages over again because they never change. The ways to apply them and adjust them to the situation remain necessary. Consider these questions and suggestions.

- Are you prepared *to be respectful* when talking to your teen? Treating them like an adult whose opinion and viewpoint you respect is paramount to a successful line of communication. You will be amazed how they will rise to your expectation if you give respect first.

- Does your teenager know that *you expect the same* in kind? As we've discussed before reciprocity is the conduit of respect. Give it to receive it. Demanding it of a teen is not your best stance. Offer it. Then make it clear it is a two-way street.

Mommy

- Are you giving your teen *your attention*? They will make you think they are not engaged, but they are acutely aware of whether you are. They sense the extent of commitment of your attention and are very aware of whether you are tuned in to them or not.

- Are you giving them *your time*? You're so busy being busy and they know that. They also know the value of your time because it's so scarce. That's why they crave it. Why they seek it at any cost. That makes it gold to them. They desperately want you to validate them by giving them your time.

- When you talk with them are you *actively listening*? Active listening is being fully engaged in the conversation while the other person is talking. That means you can't be thinking of what you want to say next and listen to them effectively. *Focus on them not your emotions.*

- Respond to what your teen says not with automatic judgement and advice but by mirroring back what they're saying so they are assured you heard them and got their message. This is a hard one because a major part of your mom job is instructing people what to do. Withholding all of your sage advice for a while until your teen is ready to receive it can be far more valuable than whatever advice you are dying to give. *Your economical use of your opinion will translate*

Same Partner, Different Dance

to them as your validation that theirs matters.

- Are you being real with your teen? This is about *true authenticity*. I have to stop and comment here to tell you I believe the word authentic is another term that has recently become overused. It's such a powerful word full of so much value in terms of what it means to your humanity. Authenticity is a tangible truth. This is character. The part of you that belongs to you until you misuse it. Everyone around you can feel its credibility and purity of intent. Your child more than anyone.

- *Don't fake it with a teen*. They can smell insincerity a mile away. This is a highly valuable asset for life. You WANT them to possess the ability to sense when they are being duped. Don't try to deceive your teenager.

- When they speak, can you discern what *they aren't saying as a clue?* Teens don't always know how to articulate their feelings because often they can't identify them. When you say *why did you do that* and they say they *don't know*, they mean it. Listen hard for what they don't say.

- Be ready to *interpret what they do say.*

    Nobody likes me can mean *I don't like myself*. *I hate you* can mean *I'm frustrated that I don't know what I can say to you to make you* understand what I'm feeling. *I don't fit in* might really mean *I don't feel comfortable in my own skin.*

- *Please try not to say they're just being a teenager.* That is invalidating, condescending, and dismissive. Don't you dislike it when someone does that to you? Does it irritate you when they tell you that what you're saying is because you're just being a mom?

- Try to *see their point of view* even if you disagree with it. This will require you to get into their mindset. Remember how hard it was to be a teenager wanting desperately to be heard and understood. Here's where mom empathy comes into play. We think of being empathetic to others outside our family circle, but it is most crucial within it.

- Remember that their point of view is formed from *their limited experiences.* All they know is what they know. Help them learn.

- *Don't discount what they are feeling.* You have the advantage of your adult perspective. You know what your teen can't possibly know yet.

- Use your knowledge to *support them* not against them.

Same Partner, Different Dance

- **Be merciful.** Know that they don't know without telling them. They will find out in time.

- Don't show your sympathy for where they are. They don't want pity. Give them *your empathy*.

- **Resist being judgmental.** It's so easy to point out their misconceptions from a stance of superiority. No one listens to a know-it-all. Present your advice as support and wisdom that works not a mom decree.

- **Be truthful.** You cannot expect truth in response from someone you deceive or mislead. Honesty is the foundation of trust.

- Do you have a clear and *mutual threshold of trust* established with your teen? This comes from prior experience of fulfilling promises when they were young. And like then, the teen years are a test of your mutual trust with all the same deal-breakers and consequences.

- Decide on your *boundaries of trust* and consequence for breaching those boundaries.

- Make sure those are clear to your teen. They need to know you're going to uphold what you say and that you are willing to enforce consequences. Believe it or not this is a comfort to

Mommy

them in times of confusion. *They're confused much of the time.*

- Know that your application of boundaries and consequences equals protection in your teen's mind. Like when they were tweeners, they don't have the strength of maturity of character to keep from getting into trouble, *they need to know they can count on you to save them from themselves.*

- Are you prepared to withdraw your trust if they break it?

- Is your teen aware without a doubt that you will withdraw your approval if they break your trust?

- Have you made it clear that if you withdraw your trust your love remains unchanged? It's imperative that your child know that your *love is constant, but your approval and trust must be earned.* This is where your teenager learns *accountability*. It is essential for their life success.

- *Offer redemption* if they cross the line. Let them know they have a way back to your acceptance to rebound after they make a mistake. Redemption is a sacred form of mercy.

- *Prepare your response* ahead of time for their

Same Partner, Different Dance

deliberate reaction to cross your line in the sand. Teens have a motto of *just watch me* in reaction to be told what not to do.

- *Teens think in absolutes.* With them it's black or white, all or nothing, love or hate. They take things at face-value without thinking things through. Their first reaction is the one they go with without considering another. *And remember those emotions they feel are super-sized.*

- Older kids deserve some *privacy*. You don't need to hear every word they say to their friends or read every text from their boyfriend or girlfriend no matter how curious you are or how tempting it may be. Being vigilant means being aware, paying attention with your full attention, not being invasive. On the other hand, I believe you are the protector of your child and your home. It's your house. They have a room that is their private space, but it is under your roof and your domain. Watch for red flags.

- If your mom intuition tells you to be on alert, then *heed it*. Do not let anything stand in the way of your right and responsibility to keep your child and your home safe. Make sure your intentions are for that purpose and no other.

- Set up standards that you are willing to *apply to yourself* as well as your teen. They already view the world as unfair.

Mommy

And judge everything in their life by the degree of fairness or lack of fairness. Don't give them reason to mistrust you as well.

- Decide on your currency with your teen. Let them know that the more they demonstrate their trustworthiness the more they earn it. That translates to more privileges and the relaxing of the rules with their acts of responsibility. That then translates into freedom. Trust me, freedom is what every teenager craves. Make that work for you and them.

Remember that you are not only solidifying your relationship and establishing a vital line of communication with your teenager and making your life and theirs easier, but you are also preparing them with relationship skills for life.

Friends

I hear moms often say, *my daughter's my best friend* or *my son and I are best buddies.*

I have a reality check for you.

Your teen child is not Your best friend.

After preschool age, if you believe the two of you are more like

Same Partner, Different Dance

best friends than parent and child, then please consider rethinking that relationship.

You have plenty of friends.

So, do they.

They do not need nor want you to function in that capacity. I hear moms boast about being their child's best friend and I have bitten my tongue many times. I get it. I have two daughters and three granddaughters. I know how much fun they can be and how much you love to giggle together, watch the same movies, swap clothes, shop together.

You are their cheerleader.

Their biggest fan.

Their champion.

Their advocate.

Their rock.

But *not* their best friend.

Now that may sound like harsh news if you had some delusion otherwise.

Here's the good news.

You will have the opportunity to be your child's friend when they are an adult and you both are on an equal playing field. Your authority will pass to their self-reliance and it will be a mutual choice born of true compatibility and consent.

Right now, be the grownup.

Take the hit.

Be the bad guy and give them an out when they need it.

What about their friends? This is a huge topic with teens. They want to have friends. You want them to have friends. Let's make sure you are clear on how to help them.

- To become a fully functioning person your child needs to form friendships as an extension of the human need for love and belonging.

- Friends are a community. It's a microcosm of the world that they can choose.

Same Partner, Different Dance

- Resist choosing your teen's friends for them. You'll see the cool kids or the super smart kids, or the artsy ones, or the athletes and you'll want your child to be accepted by them. Maybe because you weren't in a particular group as a teenager or maybe because you were and that's what you desire for them.

- This isn't about you.

- Remember that this is about quality not quantity. I know you'd love to see your child have a posse of friends and feel like they are popular and accepted. That's great when it happens but really no more valuable than one true deep friendship that sustains them. One great friend can be enough. Let them take the lead and offer your acceptance.

Please remember though it feels like your teen has been taken over by some alien force they are not immune to the frailties of all humans.

Everything is bigger, worse, and more devasting when you are a teenager. This leaves them raw and exposed to all sorts of potential danger. They are only as happy as the past moment.

Please keep in mind that they have an extreme sense of unfairness and feel persecuted often. No one likes them and everyone is against them is the loop that plays in their head. Even kids that

Mommy

appear popular and well-adjusted are always standing on treacherous ground that is ever shifting beneath them.

How do you deal with that tough info?

- *Preparedness. Preparedness. Preparedness.*

- *Be aware and be vigilant.* I keep using that term. There is no better term for staying alert. Staying alert is your best hedge against harm.

- *Consider every teen as high-risk for emotional peril.*

    Don't miss the red flags. A teenager will often send signals that they are in trouble. It's easy to miss them if you are too busy to notice or too afraid to see them. I can't say this enough.

- Consider *professional help* if you sense the situation becomes more than the two of you can manage.

Teenagers seem unaffected and tuned out much of the time. I want you to consider that aloofness, that indifference is really a cover for fear. It's easier to be noncommittal than to risk being judged. Or to risk being wrong.

Same Partner, Different Dance

When they become hyper-aware of their missteps and mistakes, they can exaggerate the effect to dire results quickly. Know that their supersized emotions translate to self-hate in seconds and hopelessness even more quickly. They have no concept of the future.

Now is their mistaken idea of forever.

You know that this too shall pass for them as it did for you, but they don't have that point of reference. All they know is what they feel in this moment.

You must be attuned to the signs of self-harm and depression.

Please do not dismiss teenage mental distress and genuine angst for harmless teenage drama. The consequences of your reluctance to take it seriously can be tragic. Meet your challenge to champion their emotional wellness with clarity and intent. Answer their call for help with your unwavering compassion.

On the flip side. Having a teenager is so much fun. It's the time when you can begin to relate to them more like adults than kids in many ways. They're becoming aware of finding their purpose and discovering their passions. They become great conversationalists if you work at opening the right dialogue. They keep you informed so you retain your relevance in a changing world. They help reaffirm your optimism.

Mommy

I have counseled people in the area of family relations during the teenager years and have witnessed many moms traverse this territory.

Your child's teen years are not your chance at a high-school do-over. This isn't your teenage experience, it's theirs. You may have wished you had done things differently or believe you are owed a better experience than you had but your time has passed.

Allow your child to live their high school years on their terms not the ones you wanted.

Unless their choices are glaringly detrimental to their functioning, allowing them autonomy is the first step toward that adult friendship you can have later on.

Failure has become another emotional wellness topic. Famous entrepreneurs tell you that failure is the only way you learn and grow. It's as if you should strive to fail as a badge of some sort of accomplishment.

To me this is screwy thinking.

Do you learn from your mistakes?

Certainly.

Same Partner, Different Dance

Can you benefit from and grow through a failure?

Absolutely. That should be your response when you fail. To access, re-evaluate, look for the lesson, and take the gift that experience offers.

If you have failure established as the inevitable and desirable it is then easy to use it as a fallback option. How many times do you hear *I'm not perfect, I'm only human?*

Think about this for a moment.

To be human is miraculous. Your brain is astounding in its capabilities. Your lungs breath, your heart pumps, you see, you hear, you smell, you feel, you speak, your limbs move, and those are all done with little or no thought on your part.

Then there are the really spectacular human abilities to create, to imagine, and to dream.

You're not perfect.

But by God, look what you ARE.

So, the next time you think about saying you're only human, think of all that you are and all you can be and all you haven't even discovered yet. Pass that on to your child. Don't let mediocrity be a

Mommy

choice or an excuse. All their fabulousness is more than enough to move them past their mistakes. Make sure they know that.

Failure like best is not a destination. It is merely a qualifier of the size and effectiveness of the effort. Failure is direction.

Those insights are your mom mission for your teenager. Give them that.

Equip them with reliable and useable information they can trust.

Give skills to analyze a situation and think critically to avoid possible missteps and mistakes. Then give them the reassurance that mistakes are useful as elimination on the way to finding the yeses.

Prepare them for emotional recovery from a mistake with perspective.

Instill in them a confidence that they are not what they do. A behavior or action does not define the whole of them. A failure though not desirable is also not to be feared. It's not a descriptor of them but of an event. The level of its power is only a variable in the equation. They are the answer.

The key is knowledge and you're the educator of your child's life knowledge. Having information and learning to discern it and evaluate it and assimilate it will go a long way to avoiding missteps

Same Partner, Different Dance

and mistakes. That's a step to success. Confidence is built on success. Even if that success is found in surviving and growing past a mistake.

There will be times you will want to give up where your teenager is concerned.

It's too hard.

But you're tough. There's nothing like mom might.

They're too stubborn.

Who'd they get that from? Show them how stubborn you can be about getting them through this the most effective way possible.

You're too tired.

This will not last forever.

That's why many moms lean on the *this too shall pass* mantra.

To do this job excellently, you do not have the luxury of giving up.

Meet your teenagers' emotional needs the same way you have always come through before. Be as careful with their fragile

Mommy

emotions now as you were with their physical needs when they were a helpless newborn.

The Band-Aids they require at this age are love and acceptance.

The nicks and scrapes and wounds of a teenager are often invisible but require your attention and the power of your healing.

You can't spare them the pain of living in the world, but you can offer and provide the shelter of your understanding.

You should tell them the truth.

This is a tricky curve on the roller coaster. You want so desperately to be a source of encouragement, so you tell them they can do anything and be anything they want. Dream it and you can achieve it stuff.

Is that really the truth?

I'm five feet and one inch tall. All the believing in the world would never make me a runway supermodel. But if I had wanted to be in the fashion industry would a strong drive to succeed have gotten me there in some major form? You bet. Are there exceptions for every rule? Of course. Should you tell them to dream and dream

Same Partner, Different Dance

big? Absolutely. Is there always someone who breaks the boundaries of the expected? Yes. Should you encourage your child to do that? Hell yeah.

Manifesting is about believing in the certainty of the possible and attracting it to you. What you envision may be less than the universe wants for you. It may be better than you can imagine. It may give you more if you're open. Tell your child that.

The greatest inspiration you can give as a mom comes from the certainty that your child will find their definition of happiness and success by recognizing and using their gifts. By tapping into their fabulousness and following wherever it leads them they will make the world better with their presence. Tell them that.

What you owe your child is the freedom to imagine. The belief that they are worthy. The work ethic that it takes to be successful at success. The mandate to be of service.

You have a lot of history with your teenager, but their story is still untold.

Enjoy your teenager. They really are remarkable. If you look closely you will see what you have been doing is making a difference. If you listen carefully you might even hear them repeating the words you've been saying or acting in a way that shows you that they were listening all along. You've gotten them and yourself to

Mommy

this place where they're really beginning to take the shape of the adult they will be.

Isn't it going to be fun to see who that is and what they do and how they will impact the world?

CHAPTER 25

It's Not Their Fault

I don't have to tell you how so much of this job is about always putting someone else's concerns before yours. You're the last one to bed, the last one who gets the new clothes, the last one who gets pampered, the last one who anyone asks about your day. Or how you're feeling, or if you need anything.

And you're the first one to give up or give in when someone's desires are at stake.

This sounds very saintly, right? Someone outside your family might even say that about you. *Oh, St. Mom, you're so good to your family.*

The trouble with all the good saints is they're dead.

It's the first prerequisite for being considered for sainthood.

Mommy

Same thing goes for martyrs. All that suffering takes a toll, then you die. Then someone notices.

Then they say, wow, wasn't she something to do all of that?

I want you to know something very important.

I want you to stop "killing yourself" to be noticed for your efforts.

Your child will never realize how much you do for them.

Seriously, I know you think if only you do enough, sacrifice enough, drudge on enough, give up enough, stand aside enough, show up enough, overdo until you're exhausted enough, they will come to you and tell you how fabulous you are and how they couldn't have made it without you.

Please don't hold your breath.

More importantly, don't hold it against them.

Remember, all you know is what you know. Your child only knows that you have always been the one they can count on.

They know you're the one.

It's Not Their Fault

The one who stands in the pouring rain to watch soccer practice.

The one who runs to the twenty-four-hour pharmacy at midnight to get the poster board they forgot to tell you they needed for science class in the morning.

The one who baked a hundred cupcakes for Teacher Day after they volunteered you at the last minute.

The one who held back their hair while they vomited from the flu.

The one who listened to their bad jokes and laughed anyway.

The one who ran carrying them in their arms into the emergency room.

The one who never complained every time they ate that last brownie in the pantry you had been thinking about all day and was saving as a late-night treat for yourself.

The one who picked up the million little pieces of their hearts when they were jilted or rejected or left out.

The one who pretended it didn't matter that they forgot your birthday or made other plans instead of having dinner with you.

Mommy

The one who flinched at every siren you heard the nights they were out with friends.

The one who prayed every day for their protection and for God's grace.

The one who hid your tears when your feelings were hurt but caught each one of theirs when they fell.

They'll never know that every time someone hurt them you felt it deep in your gut.

Let me give you an example of what can happen if you become a martyr mom. Amelia was a married forty-nine-year-old mom of four ages sixteen to twenty-four with a very busy schedule of activities and a side hustle design business that she ran from home. On paper she was doing great. Happy marriage, great kids doing well in school and life, entrepreneur, and boss mom. She said yes to everything and loved it. The busier she was the more successful she felt. Her friends marveled at her ability to do it all.

But something wasn't quite right. She felt a constant nagging feeling that she wasn't doing enough or trying hard enough and could do more.

She was very open about her pursuit of perfection and prided herself on her insatiable need to be the best. Somehow those accomplishments weren't bringing her the happiness she desperately wanted.

After looking at all the factors of her legacy, wiring, experiences, and relationships it became clear to Amelia that she had been impacted early on by her parents' divorce when she was ten. Her mother couldn't move past being abandoned and spoke often of her unhappiness and disappointment. By the time Amelia was in middle school her mother was clinically depressed. She rarely left her bedroom and was uninvolved in any Amelia's activities. Her mother loved her, but she stopped participating in Amelia's life in any significant way.

When Amelia married her only goal was to have children and provide them the family life that she had missed. She threw herself into being super mom. Making everyone happy became her obsession. When she took the bold step of looking past what she had presented as her own happiness she saw that it was based on the approval of others. By all accounts she had that. Since everyone lauded her abilities and accomplishments what could the source of that feeling of not being validated?

Amelia took the steps to discover the root of the problem. An honest look at her life revealed that she was in fact hiding her exhaustion from trying to be all things to all people at all times. She recognized that discomfort as her validation. In her intense effort to provide her children with the perfect childhood, she had

Mommy

overcompensated the deficits in her own. *Yes,* became her mom mantra and her badge of sainthood.

Further steps led her to the realization that she resented that everyone thought it was so easy for her. It was especially painful to her that her children took it for granted and didn't acknowledge her sacrifices.

That left her open to feeling resentful.

Didn't they see how hard she was working?

Didn't they know what she'd done so they could have so much?

The answer was no.

And it wasn't their fault.

All you know is what you know.

Amelia had set out to make sure her children never wanted for anything she could give, gave them no hint of her sacrifices, and then blamed them for not being grateful. They had no reference. Their needs and desires were always met. They had no idea how hard it was for her.

She made sure they didn't.

It's Not Their Fault

That was her goal, and she was damned good at it.

Then without realizing it she resented them for not acknowledging what she kept from them.

Once Amelia gained this self-awareness, she was able to lighten up on herself and her kids. She removed the burden she had placed on herself to be the arbiter of everyone's happiness and the burden from her kids to know what they could not know.

An important part of Amelia's progress was she let go of the need to make them see what she had done for them. She realized that wouldn't benefit anyone to place guilt on them after the fact. She practiced the emotional ergonomics and lightened her emotional load so she could move forward. She chose to change her view. Her new perspective was one of satisfaction that she had accomplished her goal. She had made it possible to them to receive her devotion and feel secure without obligation to applaud her. Their accomplishments became her reward and all the evidence she needed to move past the resentment and on to happiness.

Don't resent what you present.

You've conditioned your child to expect your all. Now this doesn't mean your child should be oblivious to your gift of yourself and your efforts or that they should be so feel so entitled that they are ungrateful. I think you'll find that's not the case. They do take

Mommy

you for granted. Love does that when it's secure. You do it when you take their love and their commitment to their job as a kid as a given, don't you? You have expectations that go unnoticed because you know they are going to happen. Part of the really great part of love is that it is so solid. The flip side is when that becomes just as routine, and you forget to acknowledge it.

The trick is to remind them from time to time that this is your job but it's your choice how well you do it. Remind them that not all moms are as committed as you and you're very aware that there are kids who aren't as well-behaved as they are, so everyone in your family should be grateful for each other.

Of course, you want to teach your child appreciation. You want them to validate others with their attention and gratitude. Do that by example when you interact with others. Do it in your home and give a shout out to someone who you appreciate. Take notice and make noise about who you recognize for their contributions. Of course, remember to give your praise occasionally on the things you expect, and you know your child is doing as routine.

Think they're tuned out? Try giving them unexpected gratitude.

You know how great it feels when you get that unexpected hug or that *I love you* that spills unexpectedly from their lips.

One more note, I'd like to give you. When you do so much and

It's Not Their Fault

exhaust yourself trying so hard you actually make everyone else feel uncomfortable. It sounds counterintuitive but when you knock yourself out trying so hard you actually make the people your helping feel bad that you're doing it. I think this is partly guilt they feel about wearing you out and partly about them feeling that they aren't prepared to do likewise. No one wants to be held to comparison.

Now all of that is their choice to feel.

You do what gives you satisfaction but do it with no strings attached.

Make the effort your scorecard not the accolades. I believe your child will honor you for it with their wonderfulness!

PART FIVE:

GROWN UP TO GROWN UP

CHAPTER 26

Leaving the Nest

You and your teen made it through that obstacle course! Now they're ready to launch. That really is a good term because that's what you ask them to do. You want them to bust out in fireworks of glory into the great frontier of life after high school in a spectacular show for everyone to see.

You also worry they'll burn out or go up in flames with a wrong choice.

It's the much-anticipated start-to-empty-the-nest-time.

It sounds like a cliché, but there is no better metaphor. You build a nest to shelter them. You hold them safe. You teach them to fly. You watch them go.

They have the whole world and countless choices before them.

Mommy

Choices means decisions to be made.

Job or college.

Community or university.

In state or out.

Public or private.

Close to home or miles away?

Scholarship or student loans.

Dorm or apartment.

Car on campus or public transportation.

Major?

Minor?

It can be paralyzing.

And that's just after high school graduation.

Age-wise your child is still a teen, but they are about to embark on

Leaving the Nest

a journey into adult situations that require adult decisions from a child with less than grown-up maturity or experiences.

Because you're reading this book, I'm betting you've done your utmost to prepare them.

So, let me help prepare YOU.

- Trust that you've given them the skills. If you think that's not the case sit down with them and get it right, now. Your honesty and willingness will go a long way for both of you finding what you need to get the job done for this part.

- You may be surprised at the magnitude of the changes that will happen when your child leaves home. You may ache for them in a way you may or may not have expected once they leave home.

I worked with a mom Ellen who had developed severe anxiety several months before her daughter Grace left for her freshman year in college. Ellen began to obsess over all the details of preparing Grace to leave in the fall. Dorm room décor and accessories, seasonal clothes, and all the organizational tools began to overtake her thoughts and the family room in piles of boxes.

By mid-summer she began catastrophizing possible scenarios in her mind every time Grace left the house even if it was to run a normal errand. She imagined Grace was in a wreck or had been carjacked, or kidnapped. Ellen nagged Grace every time she left the house about calling and checking in every hour. If Grace was a minute late, Ellen panicked and called her repeatedly. They fought constantly about this mom's obsessive control. Her behavior became so intrusive into their relationship that she and her daughter were barely able to be in the same room together by the end of summer.

When Grace left for college, Ellen became so depressed that she hardly left the house. She had a high schooler still at home but even with all of those activities, Ellen couldn't be distracted or consoled. Her marriage began to suffer. She lost interest in her normal activities and friends. Her obsessive need to track Grace's whereabouts long distance became a major issue causing Grace to pull away even more and Ellen to grow more depressed.

By the time Ellen started taking steps to unravel the complexity of the situation she had begun to use alcohol to self-medicate. With the specific cognitive behavioral strategies to gain perspective she was able to see that her need to control had gotten out of control.

Ellen was able to step back and see that her anxiety about Grace's safety was rooted in her fear of losing Grace's dependence on her and therefore her mom job. She had an unreasonable fear that Grace would fail to make the transition and therefore Ellen had failed as her mom.

Leaving the Nest

Once Ellen saw how her job wasn't over it was simply changed, she gained clarity to see she had options that included making adjustments for that change. She could see that the relationship was still intact and where it went going forward was her decision to make. She still had mom-work to do.

It was her job description that had changed. She was now a mom of an adult child with new challenges and rewards. The key was her mom plan didn't have to change but her expectations did. Her mission to love and protect Grace remained it was the implementation that needed adjusting.

She was able to shift her mindset and look forward to the next phase when Grace would be discovering her purpose and her passion, have a career, find a partner, make her own home, and become a fulfilled individual. They could share in those together if Ellen were willing to trust that she had done her job well so far and trust Grace to be the person they had both worked so hard for her to become.

Your child will leave home and neither of you will expire from the transition. But that's not to say there won't be other major changes that will require a shift in perspective.

Be prepared for the changes.

Once your child is off at school you can adjust to their empty

Mommy

room and having a bit less activity. You may have others at home, or this may put you in empty nest syndrome. It certainly holds some benefits to now have your time to delegate to other things on a daily basis.

Then they come home for a holiday.

Who is this person?

You have spent about two decades dedicated to guiding and leading this child. You've been giving them instructions and hopefully explaining to them your reasoning, and reminding them, and prodding them, and comforting them, and cheerleading. It was your job.

Now overnight they no longer need or want any of this from you. They've had a taste of freedom and gone from the world in your home to that big wide-open space of college where no one's watching and no one's advising and no one's asking questions. And they love it. It's like they won the freedom lottery.

To you, it feels like getting fired unexpectedly from the job you felt you did so well.

Your child's new-found freedom will require you to bite your tongue, hold your peace, swallow your pride, eat your words, and see them in a whole new way.

Leaving the Nest

It's a shock. Not just the part where they come back home for visits and want to treat your house like the dorm or the frat house. Now they have new expectations of how this relationship has changed. They want to be treated like adults with adult privileges. They don't think your house rules should still apply to them. There's no curfew at college, no one to tell them to clean up their room, every hour is happy hour, and the party never stops.

Don't let them play you.

This is still your territory.

You decide what happens now as far as your house rules and your deal-breakers. This is an adjustment period, but you can make the decision how it goes. You're still in charge of your responses. That means you direct the moment and the future.

For all the years prior, you've thought of your expectations in terms of their behavior. Your goal has to been to guide them to what is acceptable and desirable and how to act that way. Now it's about their lifestyle choices. They are the ones choosing and it's up to you to decide what and how to accept those.

So here we are back at that place of expectations. Remember we talked about how during your child's life you will keep core expectations but need to adapt the rest? Let's talk about your adult child expectations. Ask yourself the following questions. Think in terms of what direction their career is taking and their lifestyle.

- Now that you have had a chance to see your child develop a personality and temperament and know who they are as a person have you adjusted your idea of who they would become?

- Knowing those particulars about who they have become what are your current expectations about them as adults?

- Are you willing to tell less and listen more? Your new adult child craves your validation. It is possibly the most important thing in their life. They want to be worthy of your respect. They should know they have your love, but it's really your honor they're seeking. Taking the time to actively listen is a fabulous form of validation.

    Don't you like to be heard? Isn't your goal in talking with them always to be heard by them? Now, it's their turn. When you listen, you're giving them confidence in their opinions and decision-making. It signals your willingness to cooperate adult to adult.

- What are the mental pictures you have in your head about their life as an adult? What do you envision for their career, their relationships, and what do you see as their goals?

Leaving the Nest

- If the reality differs from what you envisioned, are you willing to change your expectations? Can you allow your child and their choices to form the shape of what you envision?

- How will you react if their choices and your visions are not the same?

- What is your plan for how you will or won't deal with that?

- Will you allow your adult child to form their own definition of happiness and success?

- Are you putting parameters on your acceptance of their definition of happiness and success?

- Do your definition and theirs conflict in a way that is damaging your relationship with each other?

- Is the difficulty about your conflicting views on money and status?

- Are your feelings based on your own fears about money or your need for acceptance or is it about theirs?

- Is it time for an honest discussion about those biggie issues of life?

Mommy

- If your ideas and theirs conflict are you willing to examine why? If so, are you willing to ask yourself if the reason is that you believe your definition is the only acceptable one?

- Will you look past your perspective and open yourself to theirs?

CHAPTER 27

Love the One They're With

Now, let's talk relationships again. Your child will certainly have love relationships and perhaps a life partner. This is potential emotional quicksand. All moms feel an emotional investment in who their child chooses to love.

You take this personally.

Very personally.

You love them and you will see their choice as a reflection of all you have tried to give them emotionally to prepare them to be in a relationship. It feels like part of your mom job at this point in their life.

You want to love the people your child loves especially when those people love your child.

Mommy

Simple enough.

The reality is you want to choose for them. You know just what they need. You know what and who is good for them. Maybe, but now it's part of their job as a young adult making their way in the world.

Reality check. This one's tough.

You won't get to choose who your child loves.

Now you might be saying *of course I don't want to choose for them Becki.*

But think about that for a moment. Wouldn't you really like to?

So, let's talk about this super sensitive subject. It will have PROFOUND effect on your life.

- Do you have a preconceived idea of who your child's choice of partner will be?

- Is your vision based on your preferences or your child's?

- Does your child feel they are failing you if they don't conform to your ideal?

Love the One They're With

- Do YOU feel they are failing you?

- When your child has made dating choices have you voiced an opinion on those choices?

- Has that caused conflict?

Let's talk about your answers to those questions. They can give you direction for dealing with this subject. This is the time to think about this before you have a major conflict or if you're already dealing with a difficult situation let's get you some clarity.

The first question is the same consideration we talked about earlier in your child's life. You may believe with all your heart that you know your child better than they know themselves.

Chances are you don't.

Why do you say that Becki? I hear you asking. *I thought you said I know my child better than anyone.*

No. I said you know your *little one* better than anyone.

Your child is now an adult. The legacy you provided has been a major influence, their personalities and temperament have been established, their location has changed several times, and their

Mommy

experiences have shaped their emotional wellness and given them the foundation of their relationship style.

They are a true individual with their own desires and dreams. This is what you've wanted. What you've worked so hard for and tried your best to make happen. This is a very good thing. Job well done.

But these are their desires and dreams.

Theirs, not yours.

Please trust me when I tell you that all your parenting has been vital to assisting and assuring their emotional health up to this point.

What you choose to do next is crucial.

You're entering a delicate transition that when done with conscious intent *to do no harm* will result in shaping the rest of your lives together.

Your child will make relationship choices that you will agree with and some you may not. Up until now you might not have agreed with any of them or the opposite.

I'll tell you about a mom and son who had the latter occur in their relationship with some lasting results.

Love the One They're With

Nora adored her son Alex's high school girlfriend. In reality, Kiley was more the perfect match for Nora and the rest of their family. Kiley became like their fourth child. She went on vacations with them and celebrated every holiday around their table. She was adorable and Nora adored her. They became very close. So close that Nora could only envision Kiley as the other half of Alex. In Nora's mind Alex and Kiley were inseparable and their future was a given. They dated throughout college until their senior year.

When Alex came home at Christmas and informed the family that he and Kiley had broken up everyone was upset. Nora was devasted. She could not imagine their life without Kiley in the script of their family. She allowed her disappointment to not only ruin her holiday and everyone else's but three years later she was still affected.

She began a mission to get the two back together. She interfered with Alex's desire to move on and made no secret of her determination that he had let the right one for him get away.

Alex graduated law school and took a great position at his dream company. He dated several people over the next years. I'm sure you've guessed that Nora didn't like any of them and was critical of each for various reasons that she voiced openly to Alex. He couldn't understand why his mom disliked every girl he dated. At first, he shook off Nora's refusal to accept his decision and then it

Mommy

became a source of major disappointment for him and an aggravation between them.

Then he met the girl he felt was the one and brought her home to meet the family. Nora knew instantly that Alex had fallen hard, and her reaction was to act out and behave rudely to his new girlfriend. The weekend ended badly and when Alex left, he informed his mother that he was going to marry the young woman and if pressed he would make a choice between them and it would be his new love.

When Nora and I went over the situation it was clear that she was devasted. She couldn't believe this girl had turned her son against her and she was certain he was making the mistake of his life. Couldn't he see that Kiley had been the one and if he had chosen her their family wouldn't be in this situation?

After taking a moment to step back and look at her part in the scenario, Nora was able to see that her expectations for Alex didn't compliment his. She was grieving and didn't realize it. There had been a death of sorts because her dream of her future and Alex's had been altered without her permission and was no longer a possibility. She felt a loss of control and the loss of her friendship and love that she shared with Kiley. She also felt a loss of connection with Alex in a way that felt soul deep.

Nora recognized the origin of her pain, acknowledged her

Love the One They're With

disappointment and accepted her role in the problem. There were several relationships at stake that needed to be addressed with an action plan.

She focused on the lost relationship with Kylie and her damaged relationship with Alex. Nora realized she didn't have control over his choices.

This wasn't simply about a girlfriend choice. It wasn't only about losing her vison or her friendship with Kylie. It went much deeper to Nora's unrealistic expectations that she could dictate Alex's choices as an adult and insist that he obey her wishes. This was about trusting her son to make his own decisions. It was about taking control of her emotions and moving forward to heal.

Then she was positioned to develop a loving relationship with Alex's fiancé and her future daughter-in-law. That acceptance was paramount to all involved and their relationships going forward.

Nora learned to dream with Alex not for him.

Did you get that down in your soul?

You cannot dream FOR your child.

Certainly, you can have dreams and you will and many of them will be in concert with what they want. Some will not. You can't

Mommy

change that. Why? Because you can't change someone else. I say this repeatedly because somehow you will have moments that you will think you can. Let me spare you that frustration and possible complication that will stand in your way of your best relationship with your child.

Throughout their life you will be guiding them and influencing them to one degree or another depending on all those factors we've discussed about who they are and how they process emotions. But once they become adults the dynamic shifts.

You've done your job and the time has passed with specifics as to ages, stages, and phases. You've equipped them with all you have to make their way in the world. Now it's time for you to trust them to do it.

I know that sounds great but feels awful. It hurts to let go even for the best of reasons.

But let me assure you that this new phase brings so much in the way of reward if you will decide to view as a chance to let your relationship grow. You will be wowed and even blown away at the ways you child makes strides toward becoming a young adult will bring immeasurable joy to your life.

NOW you get to be best friends!

Love the One They're With

You can relate to each other as grown-ups without the earlier restrictions.

The caveat is to be accepting of their choices. As long as what they are doing and whom they bring into their lives is not harmful then you must put your opinions aside. So, what if your story is the opposite of Nora's? You can't stand the person your child is dating or has chosen as a partner. This can be miserable, and the real problem is it can last for years altering your family life in many ways and diminishing the quality of your relationship with your child. Let's talk about ways to avoid that.

- If your child chooses a partner that you dislike, you will need to keep as much of that emotion separate as possible and not part of the conversation.

- *Words are indelible.* Choose them carefully.

- Think of words as tattoos. You can change your mind but they're permanent. Even when you try to delete them the scars remain.

- If you criticize your child's partner, no one will forget. Even if your child complains about their partner you must resist affirming with your own feelings. There's always the chance they will get over it and reconcile then you will seem like the bad guy. Your child will have trouble forgetting your comments and harshness. It will set you up for ongoing conflict.

Mommy

- *I TOLD YOU SO are four of the most damaging words you can use as a mom.*

Remember that in all situations.

If your child doesn't reconcile with their partner after a conflict issue, they need your support not your self-righteousness. Generosity comes in lots of forms. Withholding unnecessary hurt from your child when they are already hurting is true mom love and devotion.

I'm not saying this is easy or that your inclination to protect your child isn't an innate reaction to anything or anyone who brings them harm. There's a difference in you not liking them or thinking they aren't good enough for your child. Let me say here in no way am I saying you should stand by and allow any harm to come to your child at the hands of anyone.

What I am saying is you must use all your mom might to resist if it's a matter of your personal feelings only. In doing that, you're giving them far more. They know they've got your love. Give them your support.

That brings us to the possibility that you may not agree with other life choices your child makes. Sexual preference and gender identity are factors that may come into play for your mom-child relationship. These huge issues are human concepts that have to be

Love the One They're With

dealt with as such. Again, your personal preferences must take a backseat if you are going to keep the line of communication open.

Nothing severs that as quickly and totally as shutting down and refusing to have true empathy for your child. Empathy is more than the ability to see another person's viewpoint. It is the *willingness* to do so. Your sincere efforts to understand are invaluable to your child. They don't want to be in conflict with you. They don't want to fight and be on opposing sides. The last thing they want to do is disappoint you.

Try to do more than walk in their shoes. Get into their skin.

Climb into their heart and feel the tug of war going on between what they feel and what they think they should feel because they're hurting you in the process. They are torn between the people they love. They're also trying to love themselves.

Get into their mindset and understand the conflicting and often hurtful things that they're hearing the world tell them about what they are doing and who they should love. Protect them from that. Use your mom might to push yourself past your judgment to that pure place in your heart that only feels love for them.

This is more soul stuff. Think long term. Life is short is the popular mindset. I believe life is really not short if you think of it in terms of events. There's so much that happens or doesn't happen, places you go or don't go, experiences you have or don't have and people you have or don't have in your life. Life is deep and it's wide. Lots can happen and it does.

Anything you do to restrict your happiness is a loss. Any moment you miss connecting with your child is an opening for regret. Time is finite. Love is not.

I hear you saying *but Becki, you don't know this person my child is involved with or how they are destructive to my child.*

Let's get really clear. If your child finds themselves in a relationship where their safety is involved, you should be ready to help them help themselves. Domestic violence is NEVER okay. Let's be clear on what domestic violence is. It's physical harm of course and it includes any physical contact that causes injury. But it's also emotional injury. Words are weapons. Intimidation and manipulation with the threat of harm is unacceptable. Period.

You should speak up if your child is the victim of abuse and harassment. This is very different than you not liking their partner. This is a matter of safety.

So, let's talk about determining whether your mom radar is correct

Love the One They're With

when you feel the discomfort of your child's relationship with someone.

- Are you ready to accept the right person into your child's life? Is *anybody* good enough for your child? Prepare to open your mind that your child *will* have relationships and those *will* affect your relationship with your child. You get to be the key.

- Are you willing to see this person as your child sees them? Letting go of preconceived ideas about someone is the starting point. I know, I know that's so hard to do. But ask yourself how much your child's connection with you is worth.

- Will you try to find things about the person your child loves that you can focus on that are positives? Find some common ground to connect with the person who loves your child.

- Resist the temptation to nitpick the little things about their relationship or their partner. Their relationship is part of your child and thereby part of your life and your entire family's life and could be that for a long time to come.

- Don't offer unsolicited advice. You will be tempted to voice your opinion. Bite your tongue.

- Depending on their age and emotional maturity your child will handle relationships in ways you may or may not agree with.

Mommy

Your way isn't going to be well-received. Often a child will go in the opposite direction you suggest simply because they are demonstrating their autonomy and independence to you and to themselves. Remember the terrible twos? Remember the line-in-the-sand defiance? This can be that all over again with a young adult child but with way bigger consequences.

Let me take a moment here to get on my soapbox. It is our duty as mothers to stop the notion of The Bachelorette or The Bachelor as an accepted dating model. Where did we as now moms get the idea that it is still acceptable to talk in terms of "getting" a boyfriend or the goal is to "get" asked to prom or "get" a date and that you should wait and hope for someone to ask you to marry them and "getting" married as a marker of accomplishment?

It's as if marriage is a destination that says you're valuable because someone else declares it about you. We even go so far as to wonder what's wrong with someone who hasn't been asked to get married.

You may be saying *of course I don't think that. My child doesn't need another person to make them whole.*

Deep inside you've been programmed to think differently. Even if in your home growing up your mom modeled or expressed a more modern attitude society is only now beginning to shift in any measurable way. It begins with that legacy issue.

Love the One They're With

You dim their light and set their self-belief when you assess their success in terms of a relationship status.

YOU can change this today for your daughter and for your sons. Men will begin to see women differently when women begin to see themselves and each other differently. It begins in your home with your partner and what you model for your child. It begins with the words you choose and the road you walk.

These are all soul questions you must wrestle with yourself. It's up to you to listen to your heart and your head.

Then I urge you to listen to theirs in equal time.

These are your decisions.

I make no judgement but ask that you use yours carefully.

I can only offer my original mom mantra for your consideration.

Do all things and make all decisions for your child with love and honor.

CHAPTER 28

When Your Child Has a Child

Please read this if you are a young mom as well. Understanding the dynamics of being a grandmother will give you insight into how to ask your mom for what it is you need from her now.

Chances are high that your child will decide to become a parent. This is when you realize that they really are positioned to make decisions of that magnitude without your input at all. Your child becoming a parent will affect your life just as monumentally.

I cannot stress enough the importance of this shift in dynamics to your future relationship with your child and your grandchild.

Mommy

Do not take this lightly. This is a continuation of your mom job and as vital as any other.

Forget all that B.S. about being a grandparent means getting to spoil a grandchild rotten and then send them home to let their parents deal with the consequences.

Who wants a brat for a grandchild?

Are there lazy grandparents who don't want to do the work that is required of them?

Absolutely.

Are there grandparents who act clueless and ignore the child's parents' rules and schedules and practices?

Of course.

Are there grandparents who are contributing, nurturing, and viable partners in their children's parenting experience?

Definitely.

Are they invaluable assets in their children's lives?

Heavens yes.

When Your Child Has a Child

Can you do all that?

Hell, yeah you can.

Your attitude about becoming a grandparent will shape your experience as one. The happier you are and the more genuine enthusiasm you feel and can show toward your child as they become parents, the happier your grandparent job.

You can opt in or opt out.

The moment that grandbaby arrives, your relationship with your child will change.

At first, it will quickly feel like déjà vu with flashbacks to the days they came home from college smarter than you and all-knowing. They will question your beliefs and label your methods and practices as old-school. Your new parent child will tell you "they" don't do it like that anymore,

I'm never quite sure who "they" are.

This is all good.

This is the course life takes.

Don't resist it.

Mommy

Your new parent child will so want to impress you with their knowledge and their skills one minute then call you in a panic the next time a bump appears on their newborn's skin.

Don't use this against them in any way. Stay away from words or any tone in your words that has a hint of sarcasm or *I told you so*.

As your grandchild grows you may have a deepened relationship with your child, or you may find that they're pulling away from you in order to be independent once again.

If you haven't guessed by now being a mom is a dance. An ongoing dance to a never-ending song that shifts tempo and beats, and themes and moods and styles.

Where you've been the one leading, now you must follow.

Here's another analogy. Remember when you were teaching your child to drive? You spent many hours clutching the doorhandle and biting your cheek so you wouldn't scream in fear. You white-knuckled the door handle and pushed the imaginary passenger side brake. You threw your arm across the seat in a mom-reflex to protect them when they slammed on the brake?

Well, welcome back.

When Your Child Has a Child

To keep the line of communication open you will need to open your mind to new ideas and a shift in power.

Then there's something more primal and evolutionary here. Your child's instinct of protection has kicked in for this newborn.

You must step aside.

This is the natural order of things.

Do not challenge it. This is territorial and a question of prevailing authority.

This is another moment to realize that your child wanting to take charge of their own child is a sign of a job well-done by you as their mom.

Read that again.

A job well-done by you as their mom.

This is what you worked for.

This what you hoped for.

You can be resentful, or you can glory in it. Your mom job is far from

Mommy

over at this juncture. You have much left to do. I want this to be a joyous experience for everyone.

- Meet your child in a place of respect. Think of it as passing the baton in a relay. If the hand-off is fumbled the runners are limited. If the hand-off is smooth, then the runner is free to move forward with ease. It takes both of you working together for this beloved child.

Let's talk about what you can do to insure that.

- Authority is best implemented by gracious compromise. That means the best way to be the *grand* part of grandparent is to know when to step aside.

- Open your mind to innovation in parenting practices. You accept technology's ever-changing process. You think little about new inventions that come along. You know that medical breakthroughs happen every day. You applaud the latest tech capabilities of your devices. Why are you resistant to updates and upgrades in parenting practices?

- Unless you truly believe some parenting practice your child chooses is harmful to your grandchild, accept the new way and move on. Let it go.

- Demonstrate your support with your silence. Sometimes not

When Your Child Has a Child

saying anything critical is as sign of support. The most innocent comment can crush an already hyper-sensitive new parent. Your child will care about what you think about their parenting skills. They crave your approval in this as much as they did as small children in need of your validation.

- Avoid being critical at all costs. The backlash will never be worth it.

- Don't try to disguise criticism as helpfulness. Your child can sense your insincerity.

- Your support of your child needs to continue throughout your grandchild's life. They will face challenges and difficulties that will warrant your support. Use what you know and have experienced as backup reinforcement they can count on.

- You can throw rocks of blame or be a touchstone of family strength. You decide.

- There's probably a partner in your child's life who is this grandchild's other parent. What is your relationship with them? Are you working to have a good relationship with them?

- You'll once again realize how different families function when your child takes a partner. The partner has issues and beliefs in place because of their legacy. Their parenting style may differ

Mommy

vastly from yours. Trust your child to navigate these waters. It's not up to you.

- Are you willing to back away from any conflict between your child and their partner since they are both your grandchild's parents?

- Can you put any conflict you have with your child's partner aside in order to be part of your grandchild's life? It's best to get these conflicts out of the way prior to children entering the picture. You'll need that bridge to cross this road. If you don't have it in place beforehand then build it NOW.

- Pick your issues. And for heaven's sake don't make them battles. Don't be so disagreeable or defiant that your true concerns are dismissed. Stand up for only the things that matter to your grandchild's well-being.

- Don't forfeit your grandparent clout by clouding the issues. If you are critical over everyday issues, then you lose the privilege to be heard when it really matters.

- Be helpful with suggestions and offers of information not argumentative.

- You can create a battlefield or be a blessing.

When Your Child Has a Child

- Keep the path between you and your child and you and your grandchild free of unnecessary obstacles. Get out of your own way.

- Are you clear on what is a difference of opinion or parenting style and a situation that warrants intervention? You MUST speak up if your grandchild's welfare is ever in jeopardy by either parent.

- It's your duty to be an advocate for your grandchild if you suspect any harm. If your child or their partner poses any threat of danger to your grandchild, you must take that as a call to action to intervene.

- Also be clear with yourself first what boundaries you want to have in place. Decide how available to help out you'll be, how much daily or weekly time you expect if you live near, how much holiday time you expect, what part of your time you are willing to set aside for them.

- Make those expectations clear to your child. This is no time for vagueness. That leads to confusion and miscommunication that will only lead to conflict. Be forthcoming and transparent about your boundaries and your expectations.

- Ask for what you need. You are a vital piece of the puzzle of your child's life and your grandchild's. You do have rights and

Mommy

privileges that should be honored. Just because you keep the peace doesn't mean you have to sacrifice either relationship.

- Remember your child has a lot on their mind trying their best to do their job. Being sensitive to their feelings doesn't mean you don't have your own feelings and emotions that should be considered. Instead of acting from a place of hurt, present your issues as neutrally as possible and without blame. Ask for awareness don't accuse.

- Remember how this is the hardest job on earth. Nobody knows that better than you. Use that knowledge to save your child some stress. They need your support and validation more than ever. Don't you wish someone had done that for you when you were a new mom? There is nothing like mom-to-mom love transference!

It's that mommy magic that never fades.

PART SIX:

WHEN YOU'VE GOT A PROBLEM

CHAPTER 29

How We Got Here Together

When I started working with people helping them restore their emotional equilibrium, I realized that what most folks lack is basic problem-solving and coping skills. They would talk about the stress they were under as if it were the problem they needed to solve. I've been successful at helping them because I know that isn't true.

Stress isn't the problem.

It's a by-product of the problem.

Unless you address the source of the problem you will never relieve the stress long term.

I know a thing or two about problems.

I learned what I know from personal experience. My childhood was abbreviated by my father's prolonged illness and death. Without

Mommy

parental guidance I was left to figure out how to take care of myself and my younger sister. I left home when I was sixteen, but I gave up being a kid long before that. It doesn't take a degree in psychology to figure out it was the impetus for my passion for the study of early childhood development and emotional intelligence. I had to make sense of where I was to know where I wanted to go. It became clear to me that the best way to be successful was to be prepared and the best way to be prepared was to think about what to do before I did it. Really think about it. To change the view, look at all the angles, filter out the unnecessary, and focus on the big picture of what I wanted.

I know about disappointment. I know what it's like to have your story altered without your permission and to be changed in ways that can't be undone. To be handed crap to make into beauty.

I also know what it's like to just be plain old pissed off that life has the nerve to throw you a curve so big it knocks you off your feet when you were doing the right thing and minding your own business.

I know what it's like to be collateral damage in someone else's story.

I know a thing or two about stress management.

I know about being a mom figure to a much younger sibling when you're a young kid yourself when there aren't any adults around.

How We Got Here Together

I've raised two high achieving kids of my own and been a daily constant in the lives of a second generation.

I'm a mother. My children are quite different in personality and temperament. Their life roads have taken very different but wonderful paths. I learned early on there are no tricks to being a mom only some practical things that work for most and a lot of improvisation that must be done. Those have to rest on a foundation of undeniable love and devotion. Their choices have taken me places I would never have gone on my own and given me spirit stuff that fills me beyond measure.

I know a thing or two about kids.

Like all moms, my heart has some tread marks and there have been times I wasn't so sure I had done the right thing. But I do know without a doubt I kept my promises.

That's all any child can ask for.

But it's a damn big request.

I don't take it lightly. That's why I want to help make that a little less for you to carry because you're truly committed to excellence.

Mommy

And did I mention I have sustained a marriage through it all for almost fifty years?

I have learned a lot about this life thing.

This is the reason I wrote this book.

I am passionate about this to the point that it is my purpose. Let me explain. I feel those two concepts are not one in the same though people often use them interchangeably.

When asked the question, I explain my idea of what passion is by paraphrasing a quote from Sara Blakely of SPANX fame. She is a fabulous role model for all women on the power of grit and grind. Never underestimate those mighty attributes. She said when you want to find your passion you must ask yourself a question.

What breaks your heart?

I LOVE THAT.

Think about it a moment.

What means so much to you that the idea of not having it in your life would be heartbreaking to you?

How We Got Here Together

Not *who* but *what*? I know your first thought is to say your kids and your family, but we aren't talking about them in this moment.

What moves you?

What makes you happy?

What brings joy to your mind when you think of it? When you do it?

THAT'S your passion.

This can be an interest, hobby or an outlet for a talent. It might even be something you have turned into a career.

Your passion benefits you as a person and fuels your contentment.

Then there's your purpose. That's the thing that you were put here for, to give back to the world. It's a calling. It may come to you early on or maybe later in your life.

Your purpose benefits other people and feeds your soul.

Sometimes your passion can fuel your purpose and you use them both to serve.

Mommy

My passion is writing. It gives me pleasure to find the words to express my thoughts. I love thinking of new ways to say something in a way that resonates.

I know my purpose is to be an advocate to people struggling to find their way to the place they define as happiness and success.

I know everyone has problems. Everyone.

When you have children the chances for problems to come into your life doubles with each child you add to your family. Why? Because every person has problems. So now you have problems and a child with a set. Another set comes with each child you add to your world.

I know you can avoid some of them and mitigate others with your response. I know you have more control than you can imagine.

The key is in understanding why you react to difficulty the way that you do and to identify ways you can manage it. That's why we talked about your legacy and your wiring how you got them and how you can shape your child's.

Along with that you can learn to handle the stress that problems cause. Life can often feel like a game of dodgeball. The goal is to learn to be nimble enough to prevent the problems that get thrown at you from knocking you out of the game.

How We Got Here Together

Remember that the law of physics that says for every action there is an opposite and equal reaction applies to life situations, too.

That simply means for every problem or difficulty there is a positive that results. Even a problem that involves your child.

Here's what I think is the counter to having problems with your children.

Kids bring pure joy and leave it trailing behind them like fairy dust.

They can't help it. They're just that marvelous.

It's what you will call on in your mind when the going gets tough.

I believe in preparedness as the antidote to trouble. If you know it's coming you can brace yourself, hunker down, stand up, lean in, or whatever you need to do to weather the storm.

I'm deeply committed to helping you with this.

This means you need some stout problem-solving skills.

You're going to need this information not only as a mom but as a resource to be the highly functioning, successful happy human

Mommy

being you deserve to be. Remember, you're more than a mom and there's more to your life for you to enjoy.

It's a two-for-one benefit. The bonus is once you become skilled in problem solving and coping, you'll be a better parent for it.

You benefit from less stress and your child gets a mom who's got her sh*t together!

But there's an even bigger benefit to you grasping onto these strategies and using them to elevate your life. You will be doing one of the most crucial parts of your mom job.

What if you could teach your child the most effective problem-solving skills they will ever need? Wouldn't you feel more confident sending them out into the world with successful strategies to handle bullying, peer pressure and decision making? Don't you want to help them develop great coping skills to become resilient so that they can stand strong when they have a problem?

How about equipping them to be happy productive people capable of achieving their hopes and dreams?

You put plastic covers on the restaurant highchair when you eat out and make sure they have a proper raincoat when they leave for college. You recite the "stranger danger" rules a hundred times

How We Got Here Together

and tell them not to jump off any bridges just because someone else does.

Don't you want to give them this major life skill that they will never outgrow?

Of course, you do.

Let's tackle the problem and get you some solid skills.

CHAPTER 30

Start Here

You can't possibly talk about being a mom without talking about problems. In fact, that should be the first requirement to list as needed for this job.

Problem-solver.

Some days you think that's all you do, right?

I'm going to help you do it like a pro.

The first step is to get this down deep inside.

Knowing sh*t happens is your best defense.

It's that preparedness thing I keep talking about.

Make it work for you.

Everyone experiences problems.

Mommy

Everyone.

Okay you know that, but have you really considered the certainty? Instead of that feeling like Debbie Downer stuff, it's a fact that can actually feel positive. It will help you feel like you've got this.

No one is immune or exempt.

Not even all the beautiful people you follow on Instagram who live in the houses you pin on Pinterest. That's why even though you roll your eyes at celebrities when they tell interviewers that money doesn't bring happiness, deep inside you know it's true. Money can supply accessibility to assistance, and it can buy a lot of distractions to help ease the distress, but it can't cure, and it can't cancel. It can buy freedom from worry about certain things, but it can't buy peace of mind. That comes from having the emotional resilience and skills to cope.

That knowledge is free.

There's also no preventative pill or magic mantra, or secret sauce to keep problems from being a part of your life. Don't let anyone lead you to believe otherwise. This goes back to that idea you've heard all your life that anything worth doing requires hard work. I want to help you so it's not always so hard.

You just need to know what to do.

Start Here

Let's talk about the basics.

When faced with a problem it always involves someone else. It may be someone you love, or you have to have interaction with for some other reason. We've talked about co-workers, neighbors, relatives, friends, friends of friends, and so on as the circle of your daily life widens.

You already know problems happen in your relationships, your job, your family, your friendships. But you desire those relationships and go ahead and pursue them anyway. It's part of the deal of being involved and living your life. You go in knowing sh*t happens, but the good stuff outweighs the bad. You accept it as part of the deal. You go for it. The same can be said for being a mom. Why is it everyone's surprised about that when it happens?

Adding kids to your equation means more opportunities for problems to arise simply by the math. More people to consider. More problems to face. More stress to manage.

Of course, the reverse is true and there is more opportunity for joy as well. With vigilance and intent, you can make sure the joy tilts the balance in your favor.

Notice I said *your* vigilance and intent.

You get to make these calls. You're in charge.

Mommy

Problems are part of the equation.

The source changes.

Many times, it will be your child.

It's why it's easy for me to share what I've learned with you. Think of it as a tat in bright ink with flowers and hearts around it or a queen bee or whatever your trademark is.

You can't change someone else's behavior.

I know your mind gets that intellectually. You've probably even said it to a friend or somebody as great advice and it sounded so smart.

It's your heart that can't always get on board with that mindset.

You believe if you try hard enough you can make someone change. You may not believe you can change something about yourself, but you're convinced if you only push harder, or keep pleading, or continue to nag, love more, or put your feelings aside and make someone else feel good about themselves you can get them to change. That part of their wiring can only be their choice to change. You can explain, analyze, criticize, chastise, and beg. It's all wasted effort if the other person isn't willing.

Somehow, as a mom you can believe this about everyone else but

Start Here

wrapping your head and heart around your child as a source of a problem seems too hard. You've spent their lifetime telling them how to act and what to do. You're in charge of everything in their young lives. How can you not be in control of their problems? You're on top of it most of the time. How can you not overcome this?

There are strategies to help minimize the impact of problems and in some cases can help you make decisions that will avoid some problems altogether.

Instead of rules, I call my modality a set of strategies. That's such a hopeful sounding word to me. It says, *yes something can be done to make this better. Yes, you have control here of what happens next. Yes, you can move this problem.*

So, let's work together on getting you some problem-solving savvy and not lament the idea that there will be problems to solve. Do you think Wonder Woman whines about using her superpowers to solve crime?

No.

She jumps at the chance.

She rises to the occasion.

She's ready.

Mommy

She puts on the cool costume, straightens her kickass headband and does it well because she can.

You can, too.

Let's talk about it in specifics.

CHAPTER 31

Your Words Matter

Tell me about the problem you're facing. It may be about your child. It might be something in your life and it's affecting your child.

You can write it down or say it out loud.

It may be an aggravation that's irritating you, or it may be a major difficulty. Problems come in all sizes.

I'll begin by telling you that I know of all the problems in your life, one that involves your child can be Goliath in terms of size of pain.

Let's get you a stone to load your slingshot and put that S.O.B. down!

Where do you begin?

Let's start with the words you choose.

Mommy

I bet the first word you chose was *my*. You said *my problem with my child is…*

I know that feels like the natural place to start. Almost everyone begins describing a problem that way. Stop writing or speaking for a moment.

I have one absolute to ask of you.

Always say THE problem, not MY problem.

I hear you asking, *why does that matter, Becki?*

It's so important that you never claim a problem. I ask my clients not to say *my* anxiety, or *my* weight problem, or *my* depression, or *my* OCD, or *my* cancer. If you allow it to become part of your identity the problem will insinuate into your life to the point that you won't be able to separate it from who you are.

It could be something happening to your child or because of their choices and their behavior.

I know it's your child and you feel like their problem is yours. And that's because the problem they're having is affecting your life and your relationship. You love them. You don't want to see them hurt. You want to fix it. That's what moms do after all.

Your Words Matter

Or it could be a problem that originates with another part of your life, but it's impacting your child by association or by causing you to be distracted from their well-being and care.

No matter the reason it exists, call it **THE problem**.

Separating yourself from the problem in this simple way will begin the process of overcoming it. The more distance you can create from the problem the easier it will be to see it clearly. I know that may sound counterintuitive. Think of it this way. A problem causes confusion. That confusion is like a fog that settles in. You need something to cut through so you can see where you're going. You need clarity to see the possibilities.

If your child is involved whether as the source or as collateral damage you must be aware of the words you use.

Words are sacred. Words are powerful and mighty. They can create and they can destroy. They belong to everyone and can be used at each individual's discretion. No one owns your words but you. Make sure you choose wisely so that you're proud to own yours. Words cost nothing to use, but their misuse can come with a high price. Remember, especially with children, that words have a pervasive effect.

Children NEVER forget.

Mommy

What they do is remember selectively.

They may forget to do their homework, or hang up their clothes, or to text you when they're going to be late. What they don't forget are the words you say that tell them who they are, how you see them, how you validate or neglect to validate them.

Don't cause a problem with your words.

If you are in the middle of a problem, use your words to control the impact not accelerate it.

Choice words can offer you clarity to establish where it is you want to go. They can give directions for your child as they learn to make their own choices early on and for the rest of their lives.

Here's the really good news about what I'm going to share with you. This works no matter the size of the problem. It may be a small issue that's nagging at you. It could be a devastating emotional earthquake that has shaken your world to the core. You can use these strategies and make a practice of them that will carry you through any difficulty.

That's why I developed the strategies that I call Coping Smart. If you've read my book *Coping Smart. 5 Steps to Overcome the Problem & Get Out from Under the Stress* you already have these in your toolbox, so consider it a refresh. If you haven't read it, then

Your Words Matter

you need that information for being a mom in the most effective way possible. Using these strategies will make this so much easier.

Not all problems are solvable, but they are manageable. This is the core principle of Coping Smart. With five specific steps you can identify the problem, clarify your options, manage the emotions, relieve the stress, and find a workable solution. That means even if it a problem has no clear answer, you can formulate a plan of action that works for you to cope with the stress and move forward.

I think you've guessed by now I'm an action person. I can't sit back and wait to see what happens. I like driving the bus (I prefer to visualize a Bentley!) so I can choose the route and the destination. That means I get to select the music for the ride!

I want clarity. So, when I hear other experts advise people to be mindful and grateful and to deep breath their way out of problems, I get a hot flash of indignation.

Don't get the wrong idea, I know those practices are helpful. I use them as support for my clients and encourage you to use meditation, yoga, journaling, grounding, chakras, reiki, aromatherapy, crystals, manifestation, whatever brings you peace of mind. I believe the mind/body connection is the most powerful human force next to love.

These practices are incredibly helpful tools for stress relief. The

Mommy

kicker is the effectiveness can be short-lived if the root of the stress isn't addressed.

Because I like to explain, and I have learned that explanations are best when simplest, I'll give it to you in a formula.

A problem causes stress. Stress causes confusion. Confusion causes your mind to become fertile ground for doubt, indecision, disappointment, and dissatisfaction. This leads to distress. Distress chokes your happiness.

You need a *workable solution* to move forward.

All the deep breathing in the world will not give you a workable solution to bedwetting, bullying, defiant behavior, failing grades, self-harm, drug abuse or any other problem in your mom life. Meditation will not pay the mortgage if you lose your job or bring back the person you lost.

You deserve more than bumper sticker platitudes. It takes more than memes and stickers.

It takes specifics. I have specific steps to overcome the problem you're facing and get out from under the stress with effective coping strategies.

Let's take a look.

CHAPTER 32

Coping Smart.

Look at what you wrote down or think about what you said when you told me about the problem you're facing.

The adjectives you used to explain the problem and the people involved actually tell the story in terms the emotion they bring. And the emotions you choose to let take hold. That's why we talked about all those factors that make you who you are and why you react certain ways. A problem happening to different people can seem like the same reality, but it isn't.

Problems are like fingerprints. No one experiences a problem the same exact way you do. There is a uniqueness to each problem because it is happening to you.

All that matters in this moment is how YOU feel about it. How you perceive the problem and how you react make all the difference in the outcome and the impact. Your choices determine where you go from here. Let's get you Coping Smart.

Mommy

STEP ONE
Identify The Problem

You may be saying, *Becki I know what the problem is. It's ABC or XYZ* whatever that may be.

Perfect. Now I'm asking you to think about it in terms of the affect it's having on you.

Problems range in severity, length, consequences impact, and outcome. Some have little impact, others are disruptive, while others can be devastating. Some have obvious solutions and you already know what must be done to manage them. You get to decide if you are willing to do what it takes. You also are in control of whether the problem affects other parts of your life or whether you shut it down with action.

Sometimes the problem in your life is a direct result of someone else's actions. You can be part of someone else's story. It can be a partner that has chosen a behavior that involves you or maybe your child has gone off track and taken you and your life with them.

Sometimes you make decisions that bring a problem to you. This isn't about blame but discovering strategies for finding workable solutions.

Coping Smart.

I'm going to give you four ways to rate your problem according to severity. What does that mean and why does it matter? Once you make a determination of how much energy and attention it's going to take for you to overcome it then you will decide how much of that emotional energy you think it deserves.

Notice I said how much YOU think it deserves.

The theme I want you to get here is how much you are in control. You have so much power. I know that you probably don't feel that if you are in the middle of a difficulty.

I want you to know you are in charge of this thing that has you feeling so out of control or lost.

Or hopeless.

Or powerless.

You aren't LESS in any way.

The opposite is true.

You are FULL.

Full of knowledge.

Mommy

Full of courage.

POWERFUL.

You get to declare what you want to have happen next and what you want the ultimate outcome to be. You get to determine how little or much it affects you. You get to decide if you survive and if you thrive.

When you think about the severity, I'll ask you about the amount of emotional energy you're willing to spend on it. This is the equivalent of going "green" with your emotions.

Think of this as emotional conservation.

The energy you expend should equal the severity of the problem.

Think in terms of emotional sustainability.

Your strength to withstand stress, your resilience to difficulty and your coping skills are the reserves you can call on to sustain you through a problem. Those are precious resources to protect and to honor. You get to decide how much drama results.

Do you want to sustain the drama of this problem?

Wow. Think about that for a moment.

Coping Smart.

Step One requires you to do exactly that.

STOP AND THINK.

What does that mean?

Exactly what it says. Take a moment to think before you have a knee-jerk reaction or act out of anger or jealousy or hurt or because you didn't think at all. It can also mean take time to think before you neglect to do something that you should do.

Why does it work?

In the same way you use a time-out to give your child an opportunity to step back and think about what they're doing in a situation. This will give you a moment to assess what you're dealing with. What is your most constructive response? It's also a moment to emotionally catch your breath. Get a hold of your anger or hurt.

The most effective way to do that is to give the problem a rating. It's like saying, wait a minute, I get to decide if the problem is going to affect me here.

What's really going on?

Am I reacting in the most constructive way?

Mommy

Let's talk about the four categories of problems in terms of their severity.

- *Complication*. This is a problem that is an inconvenience. It can be a simple aggravation that nags at your patience. These happen to everyone every day and many times a day. Because you're a mom, the number is multiplied by a million. Your attitude and your perspective are the keys. This is mountain or mole hill stuff.

Life is full of surprises and unpredictability. It's also full of annoyances and frustration. Problems can gain momentum in a nano second if you give them the chance by giving them more weight than they deserve.

- *Dilemma*. This is a problem that is larger in scope and usually has at least two clear options. This is an either-or situation that requires some reasoning and deductive thinking to sort out. If you do this, then that will happen. If you do that then this will happen. Which outcome do you want? It takes thought-out management strategies based on reasoning and fact-based decisions to dial down the drama.

- *Crisis*. This is a problem that is much more serious with the potential for a major life impact. It isn't only about your attitude. You must use analytical thinking to assess the situation and make a critical decision to act. More than likely, it affects

Coping Smart.

the other people in your life. Your decision on how severe it is and what you are willing to do about it must be based on the well-being of those others in your life. This is *it isn't just about you,* territory for sure. Especially if your child's emotional or physical welfare is at risk. This is when the potential for drama must be contained to minimize the outcome.

- *Tragedy.* This is a situation brought on by you or someone else or it could be the result of forces beyond your control. Whatever the source a tragedy cannot be changed by any amount of action or reaction on your part. It is life-altering in impact. It requires monumental effort on your part to affect and limit the scope of its consequences and outcome for your emotional wellness. You must save yourself and your child from as much devastation as possible with very specific strategies for grief support. This is not a matter of what you can do about it as much as it is what can you do next.

Once you've determined the severity of the problem and put it a category you can begin to decide a plan of action. This plan will be based on the possible choices you have available. Notice the way I am giving you the power here. You decide, determine, assess, do, adjust, react and respond are all verbs. You choose the action. You are the lead in this story.

Mommy

Consider these questions.

- Is this problem a mere inconvenience?

    As a mom, this is the story of your life. Multiple carpools, changes in schedules, uncooperative kiddos, flaky other parents who don't do what they are supposed to do and you have to pick up the slack, rain on days you need to be sunny, stomach bugs that hit on the day of the school play, flat tires, misplaced sports equipment, forgotten homework, late night *oh I forgot to tell you I need_____ fill in the blank* items, and the list goes on.

    This stuff is a pain in your rear end. How many adjectives can you use here? Aggravating, irritating, exasperating, bothersome. The initial reaction is usually a cuss word followed by a head shake, shrug, or throwing your hands in the air. If you can stop there that would be great, but I'm sure you might have times you let this stuff get to you and you yell and you say things you wish you hadn't. You put a label on your child to describe your frustration with their behavior and before you know it that becomes a habit and shapes their self-esteem. You might even let the emotion of an inconvenience set the tone for the rest of the day.

    How can you handle a complication best?

    Is your response relative to the complication? Remember that

Coping Smart.

the most effective response may be to not react at all. What? That's right, I said it.

Consider letting the offense and the temptation to respond slide. The momentary satisfaction of losing your sh*t isn't nearly as rewarding as keeping your sh*t together in the long run. Try it and see how good it makes you feel about yourself. Plus, it's a great lesson in anger management for your child. Think about it. Isn't it hypocritical to keep telling your kids to get it together and use their heads and not model the same? So, staying calm is a double good whammy of mommy skills.

- Are you dealing with a dilemma? Is there an either-or choice to make for a remedy? Do you want what's behind door number one or door number two? Which has a bigger pay-off? How large is the potential impact? Who will it affect? Issues can be more simplistic like a car for your teen or no car. Public school or private. Hold back a school year or move on to the next grade. Or more pervasive like work from home or the office. Stay in a marriage or divorce.

- Is this a crisis that is demanding your full attention? Will the outcome be determined by what you do or don't do in this situation?

Do you need to act quickly before the problem escalates? Who else will be affected by your decisions? How can you minimize the fallout? This could be dealing with a drug or alcohol problem. A lost job. A chronic illness. A mental illness.

- A tragedy is obvious. You know one when you see it. Once it has happened there is no strategy for changing the problem. Your only strategy here is for handling the grief that accompanies it. This will take seeking the support of others. This is truly life-altering. This is devastation territory if left unchecked. As a mom, you must get the help you need. Your child will need you in this situation more than you can know. You cannot allow yourself to shut down or to shut your child out. You can't allow them to shut down or shut you out. Allow them to grieve and assist them with their journey by getting help for them as well.

STEP TWO

Manage Your Emotions

Next, I want you to get on top of the emotions that are rushing you and threatening to overtake you in this moment and obscure your view.

Let's talk emotions.

Big subject especially since your mom job is all about emotions.

Coping Smart.

Emotions measure your conscious connection to your place in the world. They telegraph messages from your head to your heart that interpret what's going on around you and how that involves you. They travel via your nervous system determining your emotional balance along the way.

You think of emotions in terms of your heart or even your gut, but they originate in your brain. It's really your brain that falls in love or feels betrayal or jealousy or joy or disappointment and then zings your heart with the corresponding emotion that you identify. That's why your thoughts are so powerful and capable of encumbering your life or enhancing it.

Step Two of Coping Smart is all about identifying the emotions that present in any problem situation and managing them.

You're angry, hurt, resentful, jealous, scared, lost, confused, broken, heartsick, disgusted, discouraged, indignant, embarrassed, ashamed, humiliated, enraged, sad.

But remember not all emotions are negative or destructive.

Emotions can also be also amazing and welcomed. There's joy, love, hope, elation, devotion, attraction, satisfaction, contentment, gratitude, and bliss.

Emotions are catalysts for human behavior. They are the end-goal of behavior. You're motivated by what you feel and by what you expect to feel. Then there's what you hope to feel. You act accordingly to achieve that end.

Emotions don't just happen to you. They are a power source to be managed and used for your benefit. Discovering how to do that is the key to problem solving.

Make your emotions serve you, not sway you.

Consider how you use your emotions and change their impact with the way you perceive them. Love can become obsession. Anticipation can become anxiety. Admiration can become jealousy. Positivity can be an avoidance. Expectancy can quickly become resentment.

Being a mom can be an excuse for not participating in the rest of your life. Your love for your child can be a crutch than enables. Your need to be loved can be an obstacle to your child's growth. Your denial of the problem can prevent them from getting the help they need. Don't deny yourself that help either.

Emotions have a history. How you have dealt with problems and your level of coping skills in terms of your legacy and how you have used them since impacts how your emotions affect you now. They can be so ingrained they are your default setting. They can be reset.

Coping Smart.

You must learn to discern which emotions are constructive and which are destructive. Emotions are kinetic energy constantly moving and shifting. They rush and then can recede. You know that feeling that comes out of nowhere and knocks you to your knees in a flash.

Remember the speed of emotion is faster than the speed of reason.

How many times have you said *I can't help how I feel?* Emotions are certainly capable of overpowering you if you allow them. They come to you, but they must have your permission to overcome you.

Emotions are not laws. They aren't fixed. You can move them, change the, stop them.

Good news, right? That hope you're feeling from reading this is an emotion. For a moment it gave you a positive feeling in contrast to the negative one that has been taunting you. Think of it as a flash of light to help you see your way through the confusion of a problem situation. It only takes a spark to begin.

You know your mind and your body work in tandem. Your emotional energy pervades both. Your body will take the toll if your troubled mind takes over.

You know the exhaustion that comes from mom worry.

Mommy

I want to help you find ways to ease that and make your emotions work for you. Consider these questions

- Can you name the emotion you're feeling right now?

- Is it serving you or swaying you in the problem you're facing?

- Was the emotion predictable?

- Does it follow a pattern in your emotional style?

- Is it your default setting?

- Can you identify the source?

- Do you define yourself by an emotion? Are you a Nervous Nelly, a Debbie Downer, a worry wart, a drama queen?

- Do you like that about yourself?

- Do you want to change that?

- How much energy have you spent on the emotion of this situation?

- How much more energy are you willing to continue to invest?

Coping Smart.

- Has that emotional investment cost you mentally?

- Has that emotional investment cost you physically?

- Is that emotional and physical cost interfering with your daily functioning?

- Is it diminishing your ability to perform your job?

- Is that deficit showing up in your relationships?

- How is it affecting your relationship with your child?

- How is it affecting your child's emotional well-being?

- Do you want to sustain the emotions or change them?

- What are you willing to do to change them?

Okay, I know that asking you to consider change is hard.

You're tired.

Your to-do list is ridiculous.

I also know that you're always going to be in some emotional state.

But I'm asking you to think about how to choose what feelings you allow to dominate.

You feel what you feel. In no way am I judging you. What I am doing is asking you to make a judgement call for yourself. I honor and validate whatever you are feeling but I know, and YOU know that if you're stressed and distressed then your emotions are contributing to your unhappiness about the situation.

What do you do next?

STEP THREE

Clarify Your Options

Now you've gotten a grip on the problem and have identified the emotions you need to manage, let's get you some options to finding a solution.

I can't talk about options without talking about that word you've heard your whole life.

Consequences.

You need to determine the consequences of any action before you can decide what your options are for moving forward.

Coping Smart.

Now I know the word consequences has a negative connotation. That's because the concept has usually been presented to you as something bad that happens when you make a mistake. You've probably used the term yourself a hundred times with your child when instructing them what NOT to do.

Haven't you heard and said this following phrase yourself?

If you _____ (fill in the blank) you'll suffer the consequences.

Yikes. Suffer.

Whew.

I'm asking you to think of the word in a positive sense. Consequences is another word for impact, outcome, results. Those all certainly hold the promise of something favorable.

You hope to make an impact.

You're excited about the outcome.

You're expecting good results.

See? No suffering needed.

Mommy

So, how do you ensure the favorable kind of results and avoid the suffering of the consequences of your actions?

You determine your options.

I hear you saying *okay Becki how do I do that when I'm in the middle of a problem and the fog of confusion sets in?*

I'm too mad//sad/depressed/lost/scared/anxious/worried/exhausted to decide.

Let's start backwards. Let's subtract instead of adding in the equation to get the correct formula.

*Begin by asking yourself what you **don't** want.*

Why?

Because of one of the most effective problem-solving strategies that I can give you.

Ready?

Elimination is half of life

Coping Smart.

YOU'VE GOT TO KNOW WHAT YOU DON'T WANT BEFORE YOU CAN KNOW WHAT IT IS YOU DO WANT.

That means you can determine your desires by taking the undesirables off the table. Mark them off your list. Save yourself some time and energy and move on to the next consideration. Big load lifted!

Next, take a moment to think of your past missteps and mistakes. This isn't wallow-in-your-regret time. It's learn-from-your-past-decisions time.

Those mistakes were gifts.

They're a huge part of the elimination process.

I'm sure you've *said I'll never do THAT again!*

You learned a lesson.

That's the gift.

Now that you've done some elimination, the next step is to find what you do want. Your emotions will talk to you the loudest here. They're the first response you'll feel. They will come to you as an impulse to react to a situation. This is that *think before you act* advice you often hear.

Do exactly that. Time to stop and think again.

Before you act on that initial unchecked emotion drenched impulse, I want you to do this specific step for problem solving.

This is a simple thing, I promise. This is surefire stuff. I call this *The Litmus Test of Decision Making.*

Think of what you want to do in this moment. Then ask yourself this question.

WHAT'S THE WORST THING THAN CAN HAPPEN IF I DO THIS?

Think through all the possible scenarios of consequences of the action you want to choose. Every one of them. Consider who would benefit and who would or could be collateral damage.

Get those clear in your mind.

Then ask a follow up question.

CAN YOU LIVE WITH THAT?

Coping Smart.

If your answer is yes, then go for it.

If your answer is no, then stop and take that option off the table.

This way you avoid making a mistake in the heat of an emotional moment.

If the outcome is that the choice was favorable, then great. You'll know you chose the right option.

If the outcome from proceeding despite your recognition of the pitfalls is unfavorable then you won't be caught off guard by surprise. You can fully accept the responsibility for your mistake.

With the first two categories of problems, you also have the option to not act at all.

In a complication that is an irritation or inconvenience you can simply choose to not let it in. If it's a dilemma then you can decide not to engage if it's not crucial to your functioning. This opting out isn't the same as avoidance. Avoidance is refusing to acknowledge and act.

Making a decision to not engage is a conscious act of self-control.

This is also different from being passive-aggressive. That's using passivity to manipulate a situation. It is inaction that is used to get a reaction as the goal.

A choice not to engage is intended to any prevent further action.

Clarifying your options can also mean searching for answers from the counsel of others. Learning by example of successful people you admire. Opening yourself to creative thinking and resourcefulness. Willingness to change direction.

STEP FOUR

Find a Workable Solution

As I mentioned earlier, not all problems have a clear-cut solution. It would be great if there was a formula. Do this and that will happen. That's not always the case because problems can be complex and multi-layered. They can involve other people who aren't as willing as you to solve the problem.

So, what then?

I believe what you ultimately need is something I call a *workable solution*. That means you have to find a way to work around the problem or to make it work for you in some way.

Coping Smart.

You can't make all problems go away no matter how hard you try.

They don't all tie up in a neat package to be tidied away.

So how do you know how to begin to find your workable solution?

I use a story to illustrate this step. It's a piece of homegrown southern wisdom from my Aunt Sue. We were all sitting around the dinner table at a holiday family gathering years ago. The topic of discussion focused on a cousin who was having some trouble finding his way in the world. Now that's code for he was still at home, directionless, and failing to launch.

After several people weighed in with their take on the situation and their advice, the room went quiet for a minute. Aunt Sue seized the opportunity to finally put in her two cents.

It was a million-dollar concept.

"You gotta have a plan." she said in her magnolia accent.

Then, there was another moment's beat of silence. We waited as she drew a deep breath and delivered her declaration of the scope of the problem.

"He's got no plan."

Mommy

This sums up the essence of Coping Smart.

You've got to have a plan to move a problem and for moving on.

Doesn't this sound divine?

You get to design what you want and where you want to go. You get to state your definition of happiness and success and set your GPS for that destination. You begin with finding a workable solution for the problem you're facing.

You know what you want to happen.

You want this situation to change.

You want the other people involved to cooperate.

You want things to be different.

You want the stress, frustration, distress, pain, and discomfort to stop.

You want to feel happy again.

Now decide what you're willing to do to get there.

Make a plan to move the problem.

Coping Smart.

- Making any plan takes effort. Resist the temptation to avoid or procrastinate. Dial down the drama by making a decision.

- Remember that timing is everything. Making a plan is crucial to moving the problem out of your way.

- If the problem is a complication, do you recognize your part and are you willing to make an attitude adjustment? This is where mindfulness can play a huge role. Learning to be aware of your power will help you manage the irritations and limit their effect.

- If the problem is a dilemma, remember this is an either-or choice and not all options are favorable. The easiest choice is not always the best.

- If the problem is a crisis, consider everyone involved. Go over your options with them in mind as you consider you needs and wishes. Plan to recover by including their needs as well.

- If the problem you're facing is a tragedy, make part of your plan to seek help for everyone involved. This is a problem that requires diligent and intentional attention. It is multifaceted and has lifelong impact. Plan to find a support group, therapist, spiritual guidance, or medical professional. There are many resources to provide support for you and your plan of recovery.

- If you are the one grieving, then pay close attention to the effects. They are pervasive and can interfere with your functioning as a person and as a mom. Be alert to the emotional and physical consequences.

- Children need permission to grieve out loud. Allow them the prerogative to voice their pain safely.

- Don't ask your child to carry your grief. If you are grieving, then they are grieving with you or for you. If the grief originates with them, then they need your full attention to help them find a way to move forward.

- Remember that grief is more than a feeling. It is a state of being. It is an entity. It can infect if unattended. If you don't work through it then it will manifest in some destructive way now or later. Use healing as the foundation to rebuild.

- Make sure any plan to move any problem puts your well-being as a priority. Assuring your emotional equilibrium brings balance to your child and your home. Everyone benefits from your happiness.

- Ask yourself what behavior you can change to bring about the changes you want.

- Who else is involved?

Coping Smart.

- Are they willing to cooperate?

- Are you willing to be conciliatory to make amends with someone if that will move the problem?

- Are there mistakes that you've made that can be useful to you now?

- Can you let go of shame or blame to move forward?

- Are you able to conceptualize that *not now* doesn't mean *not ever?*

- If you have experienced rejection can you see it as redirection toward a more favorable outcome?

- If you have experienced rejection can you allow yourself to see it as protection that saved you from harm?

You are stronger than you feel.

You are more resourceful than you know.

You are more resilient than you think.

You are more powerful than you realize.

Mommy

You are overcoming the problem with these four steps and now you need a way to get out from under the stress that problem is causing. Let's get you to the final step with some very specific strategies to manage that stress.

CHAPTER 33

Get Out from Under the Stress

Stress sucks.

It saps your energy.

It's a bitch.

Makes you bitchy.

Makes you think everybody else is bitchy.

Takes the fun out of everything.

Makes your hair fall out.

Makes your skin look bad.

It's the thing that makes a problem even worse.

So, what do you do about it?

You need effective coping skills.

I'm going to give you the most successful ones I know. This is the next step in Coping Smart.

STEP FIVE

The 7 R'S of Coping

1. Reframe

This is a concept you hear about often. What does it really mean? It's a way of looking at something differently than it may appear at first. Think of your cell phone camera. You can manipulate the result by adjusting what you see. Use a filter. Change the view. Find a better angle. Change the lighting. Add some sparkles or stickers.

Let's get more visual. Think of a problem you're dealing with as a painting you purchased for your home. You can choose a rustic barnwood frame or gold gilt. You get to choose what makes it appealing, gives it importance, or how to make it more subtle. You can design your own frame by being creative. In the same way you can decide how to think about a situation. How

Get Out from Under the Stress

important it is to the design of your life. It's a mind game for good. Not pretending or deluding but using a new perspective.

This is the silver lining thing you hear about. It's about mining for the gold in the dark cave, diamonds in the brown rock, blue sky behind the clouds. You get the idea. You get to choose the view.

2. Resist

This one is a little tricky because you have to think about a problem in order to come up with a workable solution. The temptation to replay the could haves, should haves, wish you would haves will keep you down. Resist the inclination to ruminate and focus on the moment at hand. You can do this with some of the great wellness practices that are trending now like gratitude journaling, meditation, and grounding. Get physical and go for a walk, run, bike ride, or swim. Go to spin class, boxing, Pilates, or yoga. Get your mind going in another direction with a good book, a movie or music. A great playlist is s good distraction. Take back your mind.

3. Replace

Thoughts flood your mind automatically every day all day. Think of them as involuntary as the blood flowing in your veins or the air in your lungs. The difference with your thoughts is you can choose which ones you focus on. When thoughts become intrusive, they can rapidly magnify into catastrophic thinking. Before you know it, you've fallen down the rabbit hole of impending disaster. You've created a worst-case scenario in your imagination. Here's where you can get creative. Just as your imagination can run wild with disaster thoughts, you can choose to let it create scenes where you prevail. Use your mind like a vision board on Pinterest. Put only the thoughts that bring positive emotions to mind. Then there's no room for stress.

4. Rate

You've already rated the problem by its severity, now you can rate the stress it's causing. Chances are the stress is coming in the form of anxiety and or depression. Get some distance from them by assigning a number in terms of the amount of impact. It's like when your doctor asks you to rate the level of pain you're experiencing. Examining and quantifying the stress will give you perspective on its affect and a baseline to monitor it. Give it a number. This will give you a feeling of being in control of the stress rather than being controlled by it. It will give you definitive and measurable evidence that your plan is succeeding. This will lift your spirits and build your confidence that you're managing the stress.

5. Recall

I know I asked you to stop ruminating, so why am I now saying

Get Out from Under the Stress

you should recall the past? The big difference is I'm suggesting you recall the times you have overcome a problem. Recount your successes. Concentrate on the times you have accomplished your goals.

When did you take charge and conquer?

When did you choose action and not sit back?

When did you resist having a pity party?

When did you conquer your fear?

When did you stop waiting on someone to rescue you?

When did you save yourself?

What failure did you turn into a victory?

When did you say enough is enough?

How did it feel to be resourceful and self-reliant?

6. Revel

This is celebration time again! Take any and every opportunity to celebrate no matter how tiny the success.

Every baby step forward.

Every situation you reframe.

Every unpleasant memory you resist.

Every intrusive thought you replace.

Every time you rate and quantify stress and anxiety to mitigate them.

Every past success you recall.

Celebrating releases dopamine, serotonin, and endorphins that naturally stimulate your body and your mind relieving stress and opening you to joy.

7. Rest

You're tired of thinking. You're exhausted from the stress. What you need is rest. Yeah, yeah, you know, but you also know you don't have time to rest. I'm telling you that this is as essential to you as hydration. You don't hesitate to drink water when you need it. In fact, I bet you carry a fancy water bottle with you everywhere you go. Just as you need that water to flush out the toxins in your body, you need rest to counteract the toxicity of stress.

Get Out from Under the Stress

Rest is different from sleep. You need to sleep to function and stress certainly interrupts that pattern. But rest is the balm your mind needs when it's fatigued. Emotional overload causes mental confusion and a hyper-sensitivity to stress. Then you become easily agitated and overreact to negative stimuli. Everything irritates you. Your last nerve is raw and somebody's always standing on it.

This is where I place the importance of self-care. Nothing dramatic like a fabulous trip to the spa though that would be heaven! Sometimes finances and responsibilities and logistics restrict that kind of pampering. This kind of self-care only requires taking a few moments to get to the happy place in your mind. Whatever you envision as calm. Go sit in your car, or shut the bathroom door or sit in your favorite spot and just clear your brain for a few moments. Distract yourself with good music. No money is required and no one has to fend for themselves for very long. Those few moments of mind rest will carry you through. It's also a great way to unwind at bedtime. Instead of struggling to sleep, give in to the idea of simply resting first and allowing your mind to slowly turn off. Rest to reset.

Prayer

I want you to know that one of the strongest coping skills you have is prayer. It is a way to use the 7 R's all at once. You can reframe with the promise of better, resist the negativity, replace the scary thoughts, lower the anxiety rating, recall your past strength, revel in celebration of hope, and rest in its assurance of protection.

It's mindfulness at its most present.

It's a meditation on peace.

It's the highest form of affirmation.

It's the purest form of gratitude.

As a mental health advocate, I must tell you that stress is a destructive force. It can rack your mind and eventually wreck your body. And it certainly can wreck your life if you allow it.

Please know that these strategies are meant to assist you as you do your mom job, but when it becomes too overwhelming for you or your child you owe it to both of you to get professional help.

Asking for help is an act of bravery.

It's an act of love.

It's unselfish.

Get Out from Under the Stress

It's self-love at its finest.

There are many resources available to you where you live. Start with your family physician or nurse practitioner. For your child, a school counselor can point you in the right direction.

Please get help when you need it.

Offer it to any mom you know who needs it.

CHAPTER 34

Hallelujah!

Can you hear me shouting?

I'm so excited for you!

You've invested your time in reading this book, really thinking about the questions and suggestions, writing your thoughts, sharing your struggle, considering all of the strategies, taking the specific steps, and moving problems out of your way.

You've made a mom plan, flexed your mom might, and worked some mommy magic along the way.

An author includes a page or two in their book to acknowledge the people who helped them get the book out into the world. It takes a lot of people to do that from the first folks in your life who gave you the confidence to write to the skilled professionals who do the mechanics of the process.

It's kind of like an Academy Awards speech. You hope you don't

Mommy

leave anyone out because it's your one chance to give props and recognition. Or as we say now, your flowers.

So, I decided that you, the reader, the mom in your child's life deserve the biggest shout-out from me and one all your own.

Thank you for allowing me to share this book with you. By reading it you have made my mom-at-large job complete.

I think about all of you every day.

This job never ends, and you never stop, and I know that and champion you with all my heart. The job and what it takes is so big that words don't give it complete justice. I pray these have given you guidance and reassurance and hope.

I thank you for shaping the future of the world we live in with the presence and the gifts of your beautiful children.

I applaud you.

YOU get to decide how to guide your child. They will take what you give them and will affect their generation with your influence.

You think they aren't listening.

They hear you.

Hallelujah!

You think they don't notice.

Show up.

They're watching.

You are a part of everything they do.

You are forever their touchstone.

Always be ready to take their hand on this ride and you'll both be thrilled.

You are a swaddler of newborns.

Safety ninja of toddlers.

Guardian of preschool hearts.

Homework preceptor.

Dispute mediator.

Sculptor of good citizens.

Middle school facilitator.

Mommy

Manners monitor.

Morals model.

Teenage special ops agent.

Guidance counselor.

Arbiter of common sense.

Life skills coach.

Problem solver.

Career advisor.

Launch instructor.

Heartbreak Whisperer.

Dream believer.

Their hero.

My hero.

Acknowledgements

Heart-deep thanks.

To Nancy and Jimmie my legacy.

To Allycen my sister and my first mom job.

To Richard my everything.

To Leah my amazing orchid.

To Lauren my incredible dandelion.

To Greg for loving my child and theirs.

To Presley my sun.

To Lyla my moon.

To Tatum my stars.

About the Author

Becki Pickett holds a Master of Counseling Psychology. Writer, speaker, intuitive listener, coping strategist and personal development leader, she has spent decades guiding individuals to restore their emotional balance and get to the place that they define as happiness and success.

She is committed to engaging, encouraging, empowering, and elevating parents to execute excellence for themselves and their children.

She is the founder and creator of Coping Smart.™ and author of *Coping Smart. 5 Steps to Overcome the Problem & Get Out From Under the Stress.*

Becki currently lives in Nashville with her husband Richard and their dog Henry.

She is a champion for all moms working hard to do the hardest job on earth.

Contact

To engage Becki to speak to your group or organization

Please contact
becki@copingsmart.com

Visit the website
www.copingsmart.com

www.ingramcontent.com/pod-product-compliance
Lightning Source LLC
Chambersburg PA
CBHW072141100526
44589CB00015B/2032